She's not my Granny,
she's my Nanny

Shirley Smith

ELSP

Published in 2012 by ELSP
11 Regents Place
Bradford on Avon
Wiltshire   BA15 1ED

www.ex-librisbooks.co.uk

Printed by CPI Group (UK) Ltd,
Croydon, CR0 4YY

ISBN 978-1-906641-46-7

Contents

Acknowledgements

Thank you to the WI members in Oxford who first motivated me to write. My special thanks to Joan Prout, who encouraged and supported me throughout the writing of my story. Without her help I would have floundered many times as she got me through my impatience to get it right. To Chris Prout, always on hand with his computer expertise, and to Stuart Jessup, my nephew, for his enormous help in proof reading and his support whenever I called upon him. More special thanks to Shaunagh Latymer who has done so much to make this book possible with her advice and help along the way and who has helped so much in the latter stages. And my thanks to all the children that I have looked after – without them there would be no story to tell.

1 *The early years*

'She's not my Granny she's my Nanny!' These words were said by one of the children I worked with when I was a daily nanny in Oxford, in the last eleven years of the fifty-four that I had spent looking after children.

I always knew that I was drawn to small children, particularly to babies and had no doubt about the career that I wanted to pursue when I finished school. As I wrote off for details of the colleges, it was daunting to discover how expensive the well-known Nursery Training Colleges were. However, I persevered and found a college run by Warwickshire County Council that gave the same basic training but actually paid the students the princely sum of £3 a month. From this college I was able to move on to an interesting and fulfilling life.

The years spent with children brought me much happiness. I had countless changes as time passed and indeed had to adapt and change quite a lot myself as I moved from the set routine of a training college through to the more relaxed ways expected of a nanny as we reached the millennium.

My work took me from a moderate sized house in Kent to a small flat in Oxford. On the way I lived in a smart London terraced house, a stately home, spent time in Government House in Canberra, a ruined castle in Ireland and back to smaller homes in Oxford before having a home of my own in a flat in Oxford. It was a good life, although on reflection it would seem that I had relatively little time to explore the world that was outside my working environment. I wasn't aware of any loss at the time and certainly have no regrets now. Perhaps I didn't miss what I had never had and was certainly fully engaged in the life I had chosen.

My childhood memories are of contentment and security. My parents were country people with good basic standards of behaviour and lived a quiet but calm way of life and I suspect I absorbed that in my early days. From the age of four we lived in a quiet street in Thame, a small town in Oxfordshire. Our house was the end of the terrace. It was formed from two four roomed houses joined together, so we had two back doors, two staircases, eight small rooms but only one front door. One bedroom was turned into a bathroom with an old gas-guzzling geyser to heat the bath water - but no washbasin. We drew hot water from the geyser and used an old-fashioned china jug and basin, rather archaic but it was all we knew. Most of the other houses didn't have any bathroom at all so I suppose we felt privileged.

There was a long garden beside the house with Dad's garage at the end, which served as his workshop as he always serviced his own car and would repair our shoes and do many handy jobs there.

He was meticulously tidy, everything was stored neatly, screws and nails according to size in their individual drawers, spanners and screwdrivers and endless tools hanging neatly on the walls beside the spades and forks and hoes that he used for gardening. He kept the bicycles there too, one for him and one that my sister and I shared in the earlier years.

One day I borrowed his bike while he was at work, replacing it carefully, as I thought, but the next time he went into the garage he knew it had been moved. He came into the house saying 'Well, who had my bike then?' I thought he must have had eyes in the back of his head but since becoming a car driver I realised that if something wasn't in exactly the right place to allow the car to fit easily into the garage it was quickly spotted.

That garage was a great asset to the neighbours. They would come to the door asking 'if he possibly had this or that' to do some job or other. He could usually produce what was needed and would help if necessary, often making a part that would do the repair.

One of the saddest things I had to do after his death was to clear that garage out in readiness for the next tenant. I felt Dad was watching me from above. I put a box of his tools at the gate inviting people to help themselves. Nearly everything went to a new home and I hope each tool was cared for as well as he cared for them in his lifetime.

On one occasion Dad saw an old klaxon horn lying in the grass as he drove along a country road. He picked it up, saying as usual 'That might come in handy one day' and hung it on yet another hook on the garage wall. Amazingly the door bell rang some time afterwards and there was a neighbour asking if Dad knew where a klaxon horn could be found as he needed one to build an old fashioned motor bike – Dad of course had just the thing hanging on the wall.

Dad was brought up to make do with whatever was available; to do the best he could to keep his family in good order. He didn't fuss overmuch but just got on with what was needed. When he first married he owned a motorbike on which he took my mother along, riding pillion behind him. When my sister, Betty, was born he bought a sidecar. My mother then travelled in that, with Betty on her lap. When I arrived he needed a larger sidecar which allowed my mother to sit with me on her lap while Betty sat on a stool between her knees. We were taken in this way to visit my grandfather in Wales. Dad had only £5 in his pocket for 'emergencies', but he considered that plenty.

We had a carefree childhood. There was a farm just along our road and our houses backed on to a field. There we played with the other children to our hearts content. We drew hopscotch grids in the road, made a slide when the snow came and generally amused ourselves.

There were the occasional highlights – one that I remember particularly was the time that one of our friends came along to tell us that her baby brother had died. If we wanted to see him in his coffin we could give her a penny and she would take us in to her house when her mother was busy somewhere else.

We went in very quietly, quite scared at the prospect of what we would see. We were also frightened that her mother would catch us there. In the event she was nowhere to be seen so we tiptoed in to the front room where the baby was lying in his satin lined coffin, looking as white as the satin. I thought he was a newborn baby, but since then my friend assures me that he was a few months old. To me he looked very small.

I was shaken by the experience, I had never seen anyone dead before, but shaken or not, I didn't tell my mother. I knew very well that she would have been very concerned about the whole situation.

Most of the time she left us to sort out matters between the other children and ourselves and said that we could fall out with each other if it suited us but she wouldn't fall out with the parents. Just one time though she became a bit irate when I returned to the house with five shillings in my hand – I had sold my new doll to one of the girls who specially wanted it. (She had more money than any of the rest of us as her parents were 'in business'; they were wartime evacuees from London who were different in many ways).

However, my usually calm mother visited the girl's house returning with my doll, my five shillings gone. I knew enough to realise that I shouldn't do that again but the girl in question remained my friend, so must have accepted the situation without further ado and she never asked me again if she could buy anything from me. It was a very pretty doll I am surprised I let her have it in the first place.

2 Life in Thame

At the outbreak of the First World War, my father, along with two friends, exaggerated his age to join up, wanting some adventure. He had been living in South Wales working on the engines that controlled the lifts taking the men up and down the coalmines but he fancied more of a challenge. The three young men were sent to the recruiting office and discovered to their amazement that they were to join the Royal Irish Regiment – not an Irishman among them! They were eventually sent over to France and played their part in the warfare of World War One.

Dad didn't talk much about his time in the trenches except to tell us one story. He was ordered to go into no man's land to help his sergeant bring back the wounded. He helped bring back several mates when the sergeant himself was wounded, so Dad brought him to safety. After the war it was the sergeant who was given a medal for bravery! It made a good story for us to think about, but in fact I don't think my father would have wanted a medal. He was an unassuming sort of man and didn't seek to be in the limelight.

When the war ended Dad's regiment was posted to India. The Colonel of the regiment was keen for Dad to go with them. It seems that most of the men were returning to England but the Colonel had a chat with Dad and persuaded him to go with the regiment to India. I know Dad thought that it would be difficult to find a job if so many got home before him and the Colonel reassured him that there would be a job for him as his chauffeur once the India posting was over. So Dad went off to India, a trip that thrilled him, I think. He often spoke of his visit to the Taj Mahal, which was the highlight of his stay in India.

On returning from India the Colonel did indeed ask Dad to take over as his chauffeur, a role that he much enjoyed. Dad was liked by the Colonel who relied on him, as he was able to fix any mechanical problems that arose and was a reliable driver. One of his jobs was to take the Colonel to church on Sundays. Dad wasn't very keen about going to the church himself. He told us that he would tell the Colonel that he had to do a job on the car. He would drive him to the church, go back to the garage where he could take the engine out and put it back in time to meet the Colonel at the end of the service.

In later times I heard him say to my mother that he couldn't go to chapel with her as someone had to baste the Sunday joint and put the roast potatoes in the oven. He wasn't a non-believer but at the same time he wasn't so keen on sitting through twenty- minute sermons!

Meanwhile my mother was working as house parlour maid for the Colonel's wife who lived in my mother's village; Sutton Valence in Kent. Mum had to go out to work at fourteen. She was the eldest of five children so had to leave school to earn some money. She was always interested in reading and history and tried to continue to learn what she could when she could. That way she made up for the time that she wished she had been able to spend in school. Mum had been brought up to share the responsibility for her brother and sisters by helping her mother who suffered from severe arthritis and was finally confined to a wheelchair for the last twenty years of her life.

My mother was a quiet and retiring character and I imagine would not have been particularly adventurous. I don't know how it came about, but she once had a job in London. All the time she was there she longed for the countryside. She worked in a house where most of her day was spent in the basement, except when she would go up to the top floor to sleep. Her one escape was on her Sunday afternoon off when she could get away from the confines of the house. A treat during the working week was when she was asked to walk to the post box in the next street to send a letter for her mistress.

Mum was delighted when a post became available with the Colonel's wife in Sutton Valence. She was then able to visit her family easily and was back in the country again and able to breathe fresh air once more. She was trained there to be a house-parlour maid and loved the work, which gave her very high standards for the rest of her life.

At home, as children, we always had the table set correctly, the vegetables in dishes, the water in jugs, table napkins laid in each place and so on. That was good training for me too when I went into my employers' homes and met similar standards.

My mother's parents were well-respected people in Sutton Valence. Grandad was a deacon in the Congregational Chapel and he seemed a very genuine man to me. He always had time for us and never got impatient. In his latter years he worked in the apple orchards, which meant that we always had lovely Cox apples when we were visiting him in Kent. Each Christmas we would receive a box of these apples, all wrapped in mauve tissue paper. They were as much a part of Christmas as tangerines, nuts and stockings. We were allowed one a day and I loved the smell of them as I went into the spare bedroom where they were kept in the cool.

Our house in Thame had no upstairs heating so during the winter months our bedrooms were definitely cool. We would take off our underclothes and tuck them between our blankets to keep them warm for the morning. As we only had linoleum on the floor we would sit on the beds to delay the moment when our feet touched the ground. Luckily it was warm downstairs in the living room where we had a coke-burning heater.

On days when the sitting room was used, such as Sundays or when we had visitors, we roasted our fronts sitting before a coal fire while our backs froze from the draught. I think it was the same for most of our friends and families.

During the war there was little travelling, but we usually had a holiday with our grandparents in Kent. To my cousins, who were often there as well, it was a treat as Dad was able to squeeze us most of us into his car to take us down to Dymchurch for the day while the rest went in my uncle's car. We were able to drive on to the firm sands there and use the cars as changing rooms. The sands also made a good surface for endless games of cricket.

Did the sun always shine on those holidays or was it that we only went to the coast on sunny days? I have no memory of sheltering in the car in the rain and there was very little in Dymchurch by way of entertainment apart from the pleasure of taking a trip on the miniature railway.

3   During the War

Let me take you back a bit now to the time before we were born, when my father first visited the Colonel's house in Sutton Valence. That was when he came back to England on leave before going to India and was when he met my mother. They began to spend time together but I don't think my mother knew his tastes too well as she sent him a book, not knowing that he didn't read anything except motor manuals, car magazines and the like. However, the book was passed round among the other soldiers and came home well handled and obviously much read. I still have it in my bookcase as a sentimental reminder of that era.

My parents married a year or two later and continued to work for the Colonel and his family for the next twenty years. They had a cottage on the Colonel's estate, and when the Colonel moved, as he did a couple of times, my parents and later my sister and I went with them. Eventually we moved to Thame when I was four years old.

Thame was a quiet market town in the 1930's. The market was held every Tuesday on the wide cobbled streets of the High Street, when all sorts of goods were sold, in addition to the cattle market. That caused weekly excitement and expectation as the cattle would occasionally escape from their pens and dash through the town, scattering all in their path as they were chased by the farmers and restored to their rightful place again.

We were brought up as Baptists and with many friends had a great social life connected with the chapel and with all the activities that were arranged for us. We had wonderful trips to the seaside, usually about four busloads of us, which included some parents and our Sunday school teachers and thoroughly enjoyed the day out.

We took picnic lunches with us, but to my shame I must admit that I often gave in to the temptation of sampling mine long before we reached our destination, leaving only a very small amount for lunch. I daresay I made up by eating ice cream when we arrived at the seaside.

We were one of the few families who had a car in those days. I suppose Dad would have thought that a car was a priority for him as driving was now a part of his life.

During these years Dad spent much of his time driving 'The Lady' as the Colonel's wife was always known to her staff. She was Joint Master of the South Oxon hunt so he often took her to meets where she would be united with her horse, making a striking picture as she rode side saddle while wearing her veiled top hat. The groom would see her mounted and then would join Dad in the car to follow the hunt until the kill, when the groom would collect the horse while The Lady drove home with Dad. It was always amusing watching the hunt to see the behaviour of the local lads. They knew that The Lady would throw them a sixpence to open a gate, but when they saw less generous riders coming they would close the gate and hide behind the hedge.

The Colonel and his wife had two daughters, Eileen and Mary and a nanny to care for them. It was a good time for my parents as there was great friendship and companionship between the staff. Nanny often brought the girls to my parents' cottage and the cook would come in on her off-duty afternoon and would enjoy spending time there. Being in service was good if you worked for people who appreciated what you did for them and provided good conditions and a pleasant atmosphere. The cook was a special friend of ours and she would send us leftovers from her delicious puddings, which had to be eaten or wasted in those days with no proper refrigerators. At home we had a box with a wire back and a container for cold water. This was kept outside the back door and used to keep butter and milk cool. The milkman, wearing a black bowler hat and often with a dripping nose, would call twice a day from the farm next door with milk often still warm from the cow. He would use either a half pint or whole pint measure and pour the milk directly into our own jugs. We also had the baker delivering bread to the door. His friendly chat helped the day along.

At the end of our street was a gas station. It was just a small affair but lorries carried coal there for the gas to be processed from it. The coal lorries would swing round a sharp bend just near our house so my sister and I would run out with a bucket and shovel to collect any coal that had spilled on to the road.

My sister and I were born about 11 and 12 years after Eileen and Mary, the Colonel's daughters, so we looked up to them and liked them to come and see us at home. They were always referred to as Miss Eileen and Miss Mary. My sister hated using these names and would complain bitterly to my mother about it! We also loved visiting the cook in the Colonel's house as she always had a treat of some sort for us. My father continued to drive The Lady and Eileen and Mary but by this time the Colonel had separated from his wife and moved away.

In the time Dad had to spare he took over the garden and by now Mary and Eileen were ready to learn to drive so Dad showed them the finer points until he was sure they were able to control the car. There was no driving test in those days, of course, which made it easier. Mary always drove well but in later years I remember being driven by Eileen in London. We made our way down Park Lane but at the junction with Hyde Park Corner Eileen decided that we should just turn right towards Knightsbridge, ignoring the roundabout ahead of us. The other drivers on the road were so surprised that they stopped to let us through and fortunately we weren't spotted by any policemen!

I went to school at the John Hampden Junior School – John Hampden was a local hero. He had been educated at Lord William's Grammar School in Thame. He had stood as MP for Buckingham and later, as an army officer, had earned considerable respect for leading his men courageously in the Civil War. He was mortally wounded in the battle of

Chalgrove and was brought to Thame where he died six days later.

My school days in Thame were easy. I think the teachers were kind though the head must have been strict as I was once caned for going out of the playground and crossing the road to buy broken biscuits from the small grocery shop. Not an experience I wanted to repeat. I walked to school with the children who lived nearby and soon became independent and confident.

During my last year there, as a nine-year old, war was declared with Germany and our quiet town began to change. Many evacuees were sent to the town to escape the bombing in London. Their schoolteachers came with them making the John Hampden School a larger and livelier place. I benefitted from a more imaginative style of teaching, each day starting with the excitement of ten minutes of mental arithmetic designed to stimulate us in preparation for the day's work.

Before the war my sister Betty had been the only girl to get a scholarship to the Grammar School but with our more stimulating teaching there were quite a few of us who gained scholarships. When we went for an interview at the new school we had another test to take, after which I found that I was to go into a class with girls a year older than myself.

These were the days of the Second World War. Dad was over the call-up age but spent the war years working at the Morris Motor works in Oxford where they were repairing Spitfires. He was a small man, only weighing nine stone, so was often called on to get into tight spaces to do repairs others could not reach. He drove to work with three other men who lived near us in Thame. They would leave home before 7am and it was often between 9 and 10pm before they got home again. Dad's eyes always looked very strained, as he had to do the miles home with only a small amount of light: The headlights of the car had tape across them so that they wouldn't be visible from the air if German planes were about.

Once or twice a week he would take his turn as a member of the Royal Observer Corps. He would sit in a small hut just outside the town scanning the skies for enemy planes, though I don't remember him seeing many. We were very fortunate as we had few bombing raids in our area.

It seemed as though Oxford was spared but we could see the glow in the sky from the bombing in London.

With some of our neighbours' help he had dug out an air raid shelter in the field at the back of our house. When the siren went we would get up and go into the shelter. Mum would have a case packed with biscuits while Dad kept charge of our identity cards, our ration books and any savings he might have had. They were always very concerned about the war and what would be the outcome for us all. At most mealtimes the radio would be turned on to listen to the news. We had to be quiet as they listened to hear how many of our planes had been lost and how the war was going. Much emphasis was placed on Winston Churchill's latest speech – whether encouraging or worrying – as the war took its course.

Great was the rejoicing when the war ended in 1945. We had street parties, banners and bonfires. I threw my hated school hat, which I had inherited from Betty, into the fire. It was part of the uniform when she went to the Grammar School but during the war years they were unobtainable so most girls had berets, which I thought were much better.

Before the war the Grammar School had been a private boarding school run by two ladies. One acted as the Headmistress and the other looked after the boarders and the housekeeping side of the school.

As local day pupils we were rather looked down on as 'working class'; perhaps my perception of things as I saw them. I always thought it was unfair, as we had been accepted in the school for our own ability rather than having parents who could afford the fees.

The Headmistress was quite strict about our behaviour out of school – hats to be worn until we reached our homes, exemplary behaviour while we were in school uniform, no food to be eaten in the street, no evening clubs to be joined and so on. I was a bit peeved as I would have liked to have become a Girl Guide - though I did eventually gain permission to join the St John Ambulance Brigade as a cadet. We walked home for lunch, so my mother had to have the meal on the table to give us enough time to eat it and get back to school in the allotted time. We usually were given two hours homework to do each evening so were kept well occupied as school didn't finish till 4.15 and we had to be in bed by 7.30. My mother felt that as growing girls we needed plenty of rest if we were to do well. I wonder how she would have reacted if television had been available in those days.

4 Girls' Grammar School, Thame

I found the Girls' Grammar School quite a strict establishment with seemingly unnecessary rules, but nonetheless a school that gave us a good basic education and a sense of moral duty. I never felt that there was a great understanding of children in that school. The emphasis was on doing well and becoming respectable people at the end of our school lives.

It was a time when I made some friends who are still part of my life now. As day girls we met before and after school and four of us made ourselves into a 'gang'. Josephine, Angela, Barbara and I improvised our own language and spent a lot of time in a huddle amusing ourselves – perhaps to the annoyance of our classmates, though I don't remember much hassle.

On Saturdays we occasionally caught the bus from Thame to Oxford, quite a thrill to be allowed to go on our own. I would ask my mother if she could let me have some money for the trip. She always gave me a shilling or two, but when we went to Barbara's house it was quite different. Her family owned a grocery and sweet shop. When Barbara or her sisters went shopping their mother would say 'Put the change on the ledge.' (the ledge being the top of the panelling in the sitting room). When it was time to go to Oxford Barbara's mother would say 'Take some change from the ledge', it seemed to me that Barbara was quite rich!

I envied her that ledge, but years later she told me that she envied me my home where we always seemed to have a newly baked cake for tea, on a plate with a doily, and as she said, she knew I would have a clean hankie and clean knickers for school each day while she had to search through her laundry to find what she needed. I suppose the difference was that my mother had trained in service and was at home all day while Barbara's mother was always rushing to cope with serving in a busy shop and caring for her family in the time she had to spare. I remember how she smiled through it all and never minded us hanging round the shop.

We all took the School Certificate and managed to achieve good results. The day the results were sent out proved traumatic for me. The system was that we would be notified on a postcard if we had passed the exams, but should we have failed there would be a letter from the school requesting that we had a meeting with the Headmistress. On the morning that the results were expected, Angela, Barbara and Josephine turned up at my home having already received their results as they were on the earlier postal route. We all waited expectantly as the postman came into view only to find he passed right by my house. I ran after him asking if he had a postcard for me – 'No, sorry' he said. I asked then if at least he had a letter. He grinned at me and pulled out my postcard from his bag. He had twigged what was going on and wanted to have a joke but I didn't think it was funny at the time! In the event our results were good so we celebrated together in our excitement.

Later, when the time came for me to leave school, I found that my headmistress was very disappointed that I was choosing to go to a nursery training college rather than a teacher training college, saying that I would be wasting my education. I stood my ground as I knew quite clearly that I had no ambition to teach.

As we left school to start out on our various careers we arranged with our classmates that in fifty years time we would all meet on the steps of St Paul's Cathedral in London. On the appointed day there were thirteen of us who turned up and we had a great time as we lunched in the shadow of St Paul's and then took the boat from Westminster Pier to Greenwich where we had tea – reminiscing and laughing most of the time.

Those school friends, plus girls from other forms, meet once a year in

Thame for a reunion lunch. We enjoy talking of our schooldays, looking at the memorabilia table, perusing old photographs as we ask each other the names of those we may have forgotten and catching up on everyone's news. Bearing in mind that as I write this I am eighty years old.

A Guild had been formed in 1918 by one of the girls – our reunion lunches date from that time and have continued through the years. Occasionally someone will bring along an autograph album, much in vogue in our school days. I have been often surprised to see something with my signature on the bottom, completely unaware that it had anything to do with me! In almost every album there is a drawing by Betty, my sister, usually of a lady in a fashion dress of some sort. She was very keen on the latest fashion, was an excellent artist, and would have been thrilled to have been allowed to go on to study at an art college but my parents would have discouraged her, thinking that she would find it difficult to earn a living.

In those days the thinking was that the clever girls should work in a bank to get a decent pension at the end of their working lives – not very appealing for a teenager, but our headmistress would have agreed with my parents, so there was little my sister could do in the circumstances. We had been brought up to 'do as we were told' so it would have taken a lot of nerve to challenge advice given by our elders. We were less determined than the youngsters seem to be today.

5 Nursery Training College

School days over, I went to the Warwickshire Nursery Training College based in Rugby to do a two-year residential course learning everything they had to teach us about babies and children from birth to five years old. This was my first time away from home but I settled into the work quickly.

I had always loved looking after other people's children. In my growing up years I would sometimes take our neighbours' babies out for a walk in their prams – much more interesting than pushing doll's prams. But I am amazed now as I look back to realise how much the parents must have trusted me as I would only have been about nine or ten years old.

For a while Betty had looked after a four year old girl while her mother played tennis on Saturday afternoons, a role that I took over when Betty had more interesting things to do on a Saturday. This little girl, Pauline, was used to a different way of life. She suggested one day that we should go into the bank if we needed money to buy her an ice cream! (An excuse I probably made as I didn't want her to eat in the street). To me banks were sacred places; we didn't have a bank account so weren't familiar with banks at all. If Dad had been given a cheque he would have taken it to our local shopkeeper who would have cashed it for him. Another day Pauline thought it would be a good idea to go into the Spread Eagle hotel in Thame – the smart hotel in the town – to have an orange juice. She was beginning to educate me, I think, as I had never been into a hotel. Hotels were the places where the rich people went!

At the college we had experience with small babies from about a month old, toddlers from one to two years old, and then the older children up to the age of five. At the end of my training I had the added experience of working in a maternity home doing some observational work with the midwives. I well recall how shaky my knees felt when I saw my first baby delivered – a once in a lifetime experience for me.

The main nurseries were in Rugby and we had all our lectures there but we went to Warwick for three months at a time to work in a day nursery and nursery school. During this time we were billeted with young parents and their children so we saw what it was like to have to cope in a home. The two families I stayed with were to become friends for life. They welcomed me into their family situations. I sometimes baby-sat for them and was included in their weekend outings, which gave me a break from the nursery work. I was asked to be a godmother to a little girl in one of the families, so have continuing links with her.

When my time in Warwick was over I returned to Rugby, by then a senior student, and very glad to discover that I had gained a certain degree of authority. One of the situations I found difficult in the early days of my training as a junior was when I was left to oversee the children's rest time single-handed while the senior students went for lunch. There would be about twenty small children aged between two and five who were put to rest on their canvas beds while being supervised. At first I found this a nightmare as one and then another child would get up and walk about and before long several would be doing anything but lying down while I was supposed to be getting them to sleep by the time the seniors returned!

Gradually I found ways to cope, and on returning as a senior found that the children would just stay put and would soon fall asleep. Even at that young age they were experts in sizing us up and knowing how far they could go. These children were in the residential home mostly because of problems at home, either because the parents couldn't cope and needed a break or were perhaps ill. Some would be there for a few weeks but others would be left for months at a time and wouldn't know their own parents or remember their homes. We did have a few disturbed little ones to care for which, though sad for the children, gave us experience in finding ways to cope.

In Rugby we were being prepared for the examinations that would qualify us as NNEBs – fully trained nursery nurses. We had to go to London to take the National Nursing Examination Board exams, staying overnight in a Youth Hostel. This was a new experience for me, but one that I remembered enjoying. I had only been to London on a couple of occasions with my parents as we didn't move around much during the war, so it was quite exciting.

I had good results from the examinations and an excellent report from the college. The Sister Tutor was anxious for me to stay on as a member of the staff and to continue to work under her in the children's home but I knew that my real interests were in becoming a nanny.

However, I didn't feel quite confident enough to take full responsibility for a new born baby so I took a post at the Caversham Nursery Training College near Reading as a staff nurse for a year. This was good as I was not only responsible for my own work but also for the work of the students who were being trained there.

The college was divided into two sections set in large houses 600 yards apart in the same leafy road in Caversham. The Babies' Nursing Home, where I was to work, had around 15 to 20 babies and toddlers. The other part housed six cottages for 'family groups' usually with five or six children cared for by a staff nurse and student. They lived and slept in their own cottage but went to a nursery school in the grounds each morning where they met children from the other cottages plus children from the local area. It was an excellent system that worked well and the children seemed happy.

I worked at first in the nursery with the babies under a year old, learning among other things how to feed two babies at the same time. I also learnt that it wasn't a good idea to put all the days feeding bibs into the washing machine at one time – I well remember spending my precious off duty hours untangling bibs that were joined together by their tapes!

The babies were fed with their own individual recipes according to their age and progress, the most suitable milks being chosen for their particular needs. In those days some were on formula milk but others were on cow's milk that had to be diluted and which required several additional vitamins. If it was my turn to be in the milk kitchen I knew it would take several hours to make up the feeds for the next 24 hours as we had to make sure that each bottle was correctly labelled and stored. All this work though was invaluable in later years when I had to make decisions about feeding babies in my care.

I was allowed to have special care of one baby girl there called Patricia. She had infantile eczema so had to be cared for mostly by the same one or two students. Her poor little arms were wrapped in bandages and often tied to the sides of her cot so that she couldn't scratch her arms.

I was able to take her out occasionally when I was off duty and on her first birthday had a studio photograph taken of her. I was so very pleased with the photograph, which had come out really well, but very disappointed when the copy I sent to her mother wasn't even acknowledged. I didn't know the family circumstances but was sad for this little girl. I dare say she was brought up entirely in care – I wonder where that 61 year old Patricia is now; I hope she found happiness in her life.

6 Michael and David

When I was ready to move on at the end of my year at the Caversham Training College Mary, the daughter of the Colonel my father used to work for, was expecting her second baby. When her first baby, Michael, had been born nearly three years earlier the family nanny, with whom I had grown up, had looked after him but sadly she had died when he was nine months old. Mary had taken over his care but wanted help with her second baby as she had forgotten all that Nanny had done in Michael's early years. She asked me if I would go to her for nine months to get up to the same stage as when she had taken over Michael's care. The timing was perfect for me, I was happy to do this and it was good for me to work for someone I knew so well. Even so, it was with some apprehension that I went to Edenbridge where Mary lived with her barrister husband, a few days after David had been born.

My first responsibility was to be for David though I would, of course, have Michael in the nursery much of the time. Michael wasn't an easy child. I don't think I was as experienced with him as I might have been. Michael needed to have quiet occupations to calm him down and keep him happy. I discovered that a favourite game for him was painting the garage door. He would have a real builder's brush and an old can of water and would systematically 'paint' the door with water. It made the wood look dark and as soon as he had finished one section the first part would have dried so he would start again! Gradually I found ways of reaching him and getting his confidence.

There was one time when Michael was given a storybook about a fierce cat. He was really frightened when he first saw the drawing of the very black, scary looking cat so I put the book away. That didn't reassure him as he wanted to keep looking to see if the cat was still in the book. I then sealed the page up but that was no good either as he thought the cat might be able to break the seal and he wanted it down from the high shelf where I had hidden it to make sure the seal was still intact. Making the book disappear altogether wasn't the answer either. It took quite a while for me to convince him that we had given the book away and that he wouldn't see it again!

On the other hand, David was a very easy baby, although in the beginning he didn't find life too straightforward with me in charge; I still had so much to learn. For the first two or three nights I fed him by the clock as I had been taught at my training college. He had a 10pm feed and I expected him to sleep through for several hours. I didn't want to 'spoil' the first baby in my first job. When he woke in the wee small hours I would give him a drink of water, change him, and expect him to go back to sleep again. That was what the experts had told me to do but David hadn't met any of these experts or read any of their books and had a need of his own – to be fed when he was hungry. After two or three nights, common sense prevailed and I fed the poor baby when he was hungry and learned a vital lesson that I should listen to the needs of the baby in my care!

I was delighted with his progress and kept copious records of all he achieved. I thought he was a wonderful baby and rejoiced in each milestone he reached, as I suppose a mother rejoices in her first child. In my eyes no other baby had smiled as quickly as he did, or rolled over on to his tummy, or reached stages of development over the weeks and months. I watched him with wonder and delighted in each new stage that he came to. It was only in later years that it dawned on me that he was probably just an average little baby boy.

Life wasn't very exciting. We went for walks around the village or played in the garden but to me it was bliss as I watched these two children grow and flourish.

When David was nine months old I thought I should hand over his care to his mother but she and her husband had by then decided to move to Highgate in London. They asked me if I would stay until the children were settled in their new home. This didn't happen until Michael was nearly four and David was 16 months old.

I was to find the next step one of the hardest I had ever taken. It was heartbreaking to leave those children that I had looked after virtually day and night for all that time. To just pack my suitcase and walk out of the door as though I was just going away on holiday was a nightmare. I left my very last job in the year 2000 and found that departure just as difficult as it had been with my first post. I never did find a way to cope well, but on leaving David and Michael I went straight into my next post so that I had no time to dwell on my circumstances. I followed this plan each time I had to make a change. You would think that perhaps it would be difficult to relate to another baby, but after just a few hours in the new job I would be 'hooked' again.

7 Philippa

I had seen an advertisement for a nanny for a first baby in Shalford, near Guildford. The father was an officer in the Royal Navy working at the Admiralty in London. He and his wife Susan lived in a pleasant road of detached houses with two much loved dachshunds and their little baby Philippa.

She was just a month old when I joined the family and she had presented her mother with a few feeding problems. I had the feeling that they were quite pleased to see me and hopeful that we could sort out the problems so that we had a more settled baby to care for.

Philippa was quite difficult to feed so I was glad of the experiences I had been given in the milk kitchen at Caversham and that stood me in good stead with the working out a suitable feeding plan. Once we had a good regime going she was a very straightforward baby, but very active. I remember going in to her room one evening to check on her and was initially surprised to see what looked like an empty cradle. She was there all right but had wriggled underneath her mattress and was sleeping peacefully.

Another time she somehow got the ribbons of her nightie pulled tightly round her wrist. She also ate the buttons on her cardigans so if I put her to bed in a cardigan I had to put it on back to front so that she couldn't eat the buttons. In those days we had lovely large prams for the babies. Proper "nanny babies" would sit nicely, watching what was happening around them but Philippa preferred to kneel and hold onto the hood so that she could look ahead and see where we were going. Life once again was quiet. We didn't go very far, although we occasionally went to Swanage to visit Granny.

All this was in 1953 - a time of managing as well as we could with the rationing that was still on. Things were generally in short supply for everyone. I was used to making do at home so fitted in easily with what was expected of me. You learn to be very adaptable as a nanny – each family you join has different ways, different food and different expectations of what you are required to do and you get used to fitting in as easily as you can manage.

This was a family who liked dachshunds. They had two in the house and Granny had four, so when she came to stay we had the problem of which dog to let into which room when we opened the various doors. They were also music lovers and often Philippa's father would play his clarinet causing one or other of the dogs to stand and accompany him to the music.

The parents had no friends with nannies at this time but had friends with small babies, so often there would be three babies in the nursery while the mothers enjoyed a quiet cup of tea in the drawing room. I loved these afternoons because, of course, Philippa was the best dressed, best behaved and quite the nicest of all the babies and it gave me a good psychological boost. Very unfair to the others, but I always thought the ones I looked after were far superior to anyone else's!

The days passed very easily until I heard that the family would be moving abroad where plenty of help would be available, so I wouldn't be needed anymore. So once again I was to look for another family who needed my services.

I was really sad at the thought of another move but have been able to keep in touch with Philippa's family. They went on to have two more children when they returned to England and asked me to be a godmother to their youngest little girl called Elinor, so we are still in touch all these years later. It is always very good to have news of the children, now quite grown up of course. Philippa is now a grandmother, which I am told makes me a 'grandnanny'. Having contact for so many years goes to make up in some way for the memories of my sad departure.

8 Timothy in Gerrards Cross

I scanned Nursery World, which was a magazine we all took at that time, and saw an advertisement for a first baby post in Gerrards Cross. My idea in taking on a first baby was that I could then stay with the family for years and years, caring for their subsequent children, without the heartache of having to leave so often.

I was invited to go to London to have an interview with the parents of this expected baby to see whether it would be suitable for us all. I was surprised to be met by the father, a very pleasant gentleman in his early fifties. He apologised for his wife's absence, explaining that she was unwell that day. It was strange to be interviewed by the husband but he made me feel quite comfortable and we got along well. He was an estate agent (well more of a property developer I think) building up his business again after a time serving in the Territorial Army. He was Jewish (but a practising Christian Scientist), a self-made man. He told me that his wife, Pamela, was twenty-five and had been a leading model. We discussed all the necessary details of the job and went our separate ways. I was asked if I would return the following week to meet Pamela. I went up to London again on my day off expecting to meet Pamela but once again she wasn't there. I think she was reluctant for a would-be nanny to see her in her pregnant condition. I believe she was in the flat and could hear and see me, while I was speaking to her husband. However, when the job was offered to me I accepted it, as my guardian angel was telling me it would be alright. Actually, I took quite a risk, because if you don't see the lady you will be working for and only see photographs of the house where you will live, you could be in for a shock.

The day came when I was to leave Philippa. I was feeling acutely miserable as I caught a train to Waterloo to go to the nursing home near Harley Street where Timothy had been born five days earlier. There I met my new employer for the first time. She was sitting in a chair, looking the model from top to toe - in the way she sat, the way she wore her clothes, her beautifully manicured nails and well groomed hair. I worked for her for eight years and she always looked the same with not a hair out of place.

She was quite a formal lady. Perhaps she felt as nervous as I did. She insisted on calling me Miss Smith. I've never thought that Smith was an ideal name to be blessed with so asked her if she could call me Nanny as that was what everyone else had called me. She didn't seem to be able to do that for the time being – we had to get to know each other better before I became Nanny. We made rather polite conversation while we were in the nursing home as the parents filled me in on Timothy's first few days. He looked a very peaceful baby and I was hoping we would become friends as we got to know each other in the coming days.

After a while we left for Gerrards Cross in Buckinghamshire in a chauffeur driven Bentley, so I guessed that my days of making do and mending were over. We came to a very pleasant house set in a quiet area of Gerrards Cross. It wasn't large but had plenty of room for us all. There was a resident cook who had been with the family for a while. Everything in the house seemed to be colour co-ordinated. I had a lovely gabled room with matching glazed chintz dressing table, curtains, bedcover, etc. and Timothy's room was a delight, with nursery furniture painted with animals and every drawer and cupboard filled with baby clothes. I think that Harrods had persuaded Pamela that she needed plenty of everything. One cupboard held nine dozen nappies as I was expected to send the nappies to the laundry, but I said I was quite happy to use the automatic washing machine I had seen in the kitchen (not many homes had one in 1953). I didn't add that I had boiled David and Philippa's nappies in a bucket on the kitchen stove; I didn't want to let the side down!

Timothy was a lovely, settled little baby and we soon got into our nursery routine but it was a little while before I felt settled in the home. Fortunately the family's jolly cook and I soon became friends, sharing a sitting room in the evenings. At the beginning I was expected to join Timothy's parents at dinner time, which I found an ordeal as the meal went on for a long while and my precious evening time was disappearing fast. As a nanny the evenings are the only time you have to yourself to wash your hair, or do your knitting, or write letters – something that we all did in those days – but I realised that Timothy's mother was just trying to make me feel one of the family. She didn't really know what made nannies tick. There was no reason why she should as her life had been spent in the modelling world, in London life and all that that meant. I don't think she had had anything to do with small babies and what they entailed. She reluctantly agreed to let me collect my supper from the kitchen and to have it in the nursery, which suited me much better and I am sure it was much better for the parents to have their privacy at the end of their day.

It was then that I realised that there was quite a gap between the world in which the parents lived and the nursery world that I knew. I would have to find a way for Timothy to be happy in both worlds, which we did eventually achieve as he grew to be a little boy.

Life in Gerrards Cross was quiet but happy. Timothy spent his mornings in the garden in his pram and in the afternoons we walked around the village entertaining each other. Sometimes we would go to Hove for the weekend where the parents had a flat. Each April Timothy and I would be taken to the Royal Bath Hotel in Bournemouth while the cook had a holiday and the parents went abroad.

I loved this time, much of which was spent in the hotel nursery with the resident nursery nurse and any children who were staying in the hotel. No children under six were allowed in the main dining room so the children all ate and played in the nursery, sometimes with their nannies but often on their own, so I would find myself helping with them at mealtimes and sometimes listening out for them in the evenings as the children were all on the same corridor.

We were quite free to do whatever we liked there so we spent time exploring all that was interesting for Timothy and of course enjoyed the sea and the beach.

I felt a different sort of freedom there in Bournemouth. It wasn't that I did anything very different with Timothy but I was never completely at my ease with Pamela. I know that she wasn't able to trust me. She told me once that she had been brought up to spy on the maid that her mother had employed, to tell her mother what the maid did when they were on their own. I imagine this had rubbed off on Pamela and accounted for her suspicions of anyone who worked for her.

While we were in Gerrards Cross she and her husband would spend one night a week in their flat in London. They would ring me to say when we could expect them home. However, on one occasion Pamela rang at about 7pm to say they would be back at the usual time around 9.30, this was the weekly routine - but five minutes after the call on that particular evening the front door opened and in they came. 'Surprise, surprise' she said, 'We rang you from the Bull Hotel at the bottom of the road.' I honestly don't know what they thought I would be doing in her absence but she found me as usual having supper with the cook in our sitting room.

That sort of treatment didn't make me feel very good and left a nasty taste in my mouth. It wasn't the easiest way to foster a good relationship and left me feeling rather wary of her, as I didn't know what to expect in any given situation.

9 Timothy in London

Timothy's parents had given the early years in the country to Timothy but they really missed the London life. Timothy's father had had to commute every day and his mother would spend one night a week in London. They missed the social life and all their interests in London, so they decided to move when Timothy was three.

They bought a mews house just off Belgrave Square and if I had thought that the Gerrards Cross house was rather formal this was even more so. Absolutely everything was colour-coordinated, but the drawing room was particularly formal. I was always aware that I might squash a cushion or move a magazine out of place and the nursery on the top floor was expected to look spick and span at all times. A Portuguese couple were employed to run the house as cook and butler so we were well into the feel of a London house albeit on a small scale.

We were near enough to spend some time on our walks watching the Changing of the Guards ceremony at Buckingham Palace. Timothy used to enjoy the bands and like many other small boys would march along in time to the music. We saw the rehearsal for Princess Margaret's wedding. Timothy's mother wouldn't have liked us to go down among the crowds on the actual wedding day. She suggested that I should invite one of Timothy's friends and his nanny to lunch on that day so that the children could play together and Nanny and I could watch the wedding on television. Pamela and her husband were on holiday abroad at that time.

Once again I knew I was being checked on. Pamela always rang us in the evenings to speak to Timothy and see how we were, but on Princess Margaret's wedding day she rang at lunchtime. She asked what were doing and feigned surprise when I told her we had friends to lunch so that we could enjoy the wedding. 'Oh, was it today? She said!!

It was here that I met the London nannies for the first time. They were quite a formidable bunch of ladies but like any other group, once we had got to know each other I found them friendly and good company, which was important as a nanny's life can be quite lonely. We would meet in Hyde Park or Kensington Gardens and sit and chat while the children played with each other. Timothy wore tailored coats with matching shorts, a velvet cap to match the collar of his coat and polished shoes. I often took an extra pair of trousers with me and a sponge bag so that I could change Timothy and leave him free to play cowboys and Indians or whatever the game of the day was. Then I would tidy him up to walk back home through Knightsbridge.

Timothy was a quiet and rather reserved child so I was glad of this opportunity for him to have other children to play with and whose company he could enjoy. Of course, there was little I could do to change his nature but as his nanny it was up to me to encourage him to be as self-confident as I could and he gradually learned to enjoy playing with the other children. Much was expected of him from his mother. She told me one day that all she wanted was that he behaved like a small adult. He wasn't yet four. I tried to explain that he needed to be a child first but my views were discounted.

Once a week we would go to Miss Betty Vacani's well known dancing class where the children would be put through their paces. I think they seemed to enjoy it and it gave them the experience of getting a little discipline from someone outside the family and the opportunity to work together and take their place with other children. This was something that children nowadays get used to in playgroups and pre-school groups but these weren't generally available in the fifties.

10 Travels in Europe

When Timothy was five he went to a school in Eaton Square, which he enjoyed. He was never going to be at the front of any class activity, he much preferred to follow others, but he was a very capable child, had several good friends, enjoyed what school had to offer and was quick at understanding what was expected of him. He soon learned to read and write and was well away.

At this time his parents decided that he was old enough to go on holiday with them, so our days in Bournemouth came to an end. Instead we went to first class hotels such as the Palace Hotel in St Moritz and the Carlton in Cannes. My friends were green with envy but to be honest, they weren't always the easiest places to be with a small child who often had to be seen but not heard.

In St Moritz, Timothy wasn't allowed to learn to ski but we would take the lift up to the ski slope and I would toboggan down with him into the town. We would watch ice hockey matches, admire ice sculptures being carved, and generally amuse ourselves. We would meet the parents for lunch, often in a conservatory or somewhere away from the adult guests. Then in the evenings, when things were going on outside, I would have a meal with Timothy in our rooms and then spend the evening upstairs doing my own thing while Timothy slept. My friends thought I would be having an exciting time but we were on the fringe of any excitement that was happening around us.

In Cannes, the beach owned by the hotel was raked over every morning by the staff before the guests went out with their newspapers and drinks to enjoy the sea and beach. It would have been sacrilege for Timothy to actually dig a hole in that sand. I usually took him along to the public beach where he would find other children to play with and where he could dig to his heart's desire.

It was a great privilege for me to see what life was like in such places and I was grateful for that opportunity, though I must admit that sometimes I felt out of my comfort zone. That was something that a nanny had to experience and learn from because each time you change jobs your whole life changes, where you live, what you eat, where you go and who you meet – you can never know what lies round the next corner.

I very rarely took Timothy out away from London on my own as our expeditions were organised for us and we went with the chauffeur. but there was one occasion when we were allowed to go by train from London to Princes Risborough to visit my sister and her family.

I explained to Timothy that my sister and her husband lived in a small but very nice house in the country, that they had a baby boy called Stuart, and that they didn't have as much money as most of the people Timothy had met. We duly arrived at the station and made our way to my sister's house. Timothy was delighted with it as he could go straight out into the garden through the French doors and back in again, quite different for a child who was used to living on the second floor of a London house with no garden.

After a while he came to me and said 'I have seen the baby and his daddy and the cook but where is your sister? I had to explain that the lady cooking the lunch was indeed my sister and they didn't actually have a cook – what a strange thing!

As lunchtime approached, my brother-in-law asked Timothy if he liked ice cream and if he would like to go with him to the shop to buy some. He then took out his small change pretending he had to make quite sure he had enough money to pay for it, and off they went. On the way home in the train Timothy said that he didn't think that my sister was really very poor because they had quite enough money for the ice cream and even some left over afterwards! It was a small glimpse for him into another world, which he had thoroughly enjoyed. I wished I could have taken him home with me more often.

The years passed all too quickly and the time was drawing near when Timothy would be eight and ready to go to boarding school. He knew that this was the plan as all his friends were going away to school at eight, but I was aware that he might find it a big step to take. He had grown in confidence through the years but was still not the sort of boy who would find boarding school exactly to his liking. I tried to prepare him as well as I could. We talked about it all a lot and I told him that he would always be able to see me because wherever I was with my next family he could always come to visit – explaining that any child I looked after would be special to me for always.

Timothy's mother had broken her collarbone so wanted me to stay on for a week or two after Timothy had gone to school, to give her a hand. It was a long day when his parents drove him down to Sussex to his new school, but they eventually returned in the early evening. They came straight up to the nursery to tell me how he had got on, bringing with them a bottle of champagne to drink Timothy's health. It wasn't that they were glad he had gone to school. They loved their little boy and had done everything they could to make his life happy but they were just so glad that his 'nursery days' were over. I don't like champagne at the best of times but if I had known then that I wouldn't be allowed to see Timothy for the next 15 years I would have been devastated, but I was spared that knowledge at the time.

11 Moving on

Knowing that Timothy was due to go to boarding school I had been looking for another post to follow on to and had been invited to an interview with a very young mother who was expecting her first baby. She lived with her husband in Smith Street in Chelsea. I had a lot of friends in London at this time and was looking for a position where I could continue to meet them.

After the interview I was offered the job. I was to be working for Elizabeth, the eldest of five children of a titled family. She was only twenty and was married to Oliver, a thirty year old stockbroker, working in the City. He was a member of an Anglo-Irish family who owned Blarney Castle in County Cork in Ireland. When I was offered the post as their Nanny I was delighted because I had liked them at the interview and thought we could work together well. Elizabeth was the eldest of five children. As her youngest sister Lucy was only seven at that time and still had the family Nanny to care for her, I knew that she would be familiar with the ways of nannies and the running of a nursery.

However, just a few weeks before Timothy went to school Elizabeth rang me and asked if I would be prepared to work for her if the job was in the country, rather than in London. She went on to explain that her father, Viscount De L'Isle, had been appointed as Governor General to Australia, which would mean that he and Lady De L'Isle and their youngest four children would be going to Australia for four years. During that time he wanted Elizabeth to run his country house for him – hence the need to live in the country.

Elizabeth went on to explain that the house was indeed a stately home; Penshurst Place near Tonbridge in Kent. So suddenly the picture was enlarging before my eyes as I was being asked if I would like to live and work in a stately home that was open to the public, and also being asked if I would be prepared to take the baby to Australia for her first Christmas when she would be seven months old, not questions I had ever been asked before. By this time, my guardian angel was nudging me in the back, and although it seemed a rather daunting prospect, it had the promise of being somewhat more exciting than the usual routine of walks in Hyde Park and Kensington Gardens. So with only a few moments hesitation, I accepted the challenge. I have always felt that we have a guardian angel who steers or nudges us along the way we should go and it had seemed so whenever I had to make a decision about a new post – especially so at this time when I might possibly have wondered if the challenge was going to be too problematic.

During this time Timothy was beginning to write some of the many letters he sent from school. His parents had told him that now he was eight he shouldn't call me Nanny. That was a title small people used and he was now grown up but the poor child was confused and didn't know what to call me. Each time I wrote to him I enclosed a self-addressed envelope, addressed to me as Miss S M Smith, so all he could think of was that he should write to me with that name. I have letters from him, all starting Dear S M Smith!!

He wrote asking me to send him the cricket scores from the paper, telling me of his activities at school and asking me about the new baby I was looking after and sending drawings of rockets, which interested him at the time. I still have some of these letters one saying – "Once I got ten sums right?" and another "Don't forget that when I am eighteen I will look after you for the rest of your life"!

12 Shaunagh

Three weeks after Timothy went to his boarding school Elizabeth's husband Oliver rang to let me know that Shaunagh had been born. As their maternity nurse had to leave to go to her next post, he asked me if I could start work with them straight away.

I went to their house in Smith Street in Chelsea to meet Shaunagh for the first time and even if you don't like babies you would have loved Shaunagh. She was really pretty, very calm and a perfect English baby with bright eyes, an enquiring look, pink cheeks and a very knowing feel about her. I was badly missing Timothy and hadn't had a baby to care for since he was small, eight years previously, so I suppose I was more than ready to be hooked once again!

I was made very welcome by Elizabeth, and on my first evening there I was asked if I would collect my supper from the kitchen. So I knew that we all knew that it was a far better arrangement for nannies to eat their evening meal in the nursery and for parents to enjoy their own company in the dining room. I breathed a great sigh of relief as I understood that I was back in the upstairs downstairs situation that I had experienced when I was growing up. I had seen how the relationships between the family and their staff made a perfectly acceptable balance. It's a system that worked well in its day.

Life when caring for Shaunagh was very good. The family employed a cook whose small daughter spent some time in the nursery with us when her mother was busy in the kitchen. When Shaunagh was three weeks

old, Lady De L'Isle, her Granny, arrived to drive us down to Penshurst
Place for the weekend. As we approached the house, which can be seen
from the road, I just couldn't believe that this would be my home for the
next four years. It is a truly beautiful house set in parkland with a ha-ha
separating it from the road. It was given by Edward VI to his steward and
tutor, Sir William Sidney. His son Henry married Lady Mary Dudley, a
relation of the famous Robert Dudley, the Earl of Leicester, said to be
a great love of Queen Elizabeth. Their son, Sir Philip Sidney, the poet
courtier and soldier was born at Penshurst. The house has been a home
for the Sidney family since that time, although it went into some decline
during the Second World War. When Shaunagh's grandfather inherited
it as Lord De L'Isle and Dudley he made great plans to restore it to its
original condition in order to open it to the public and make it a thriving
business.

As I entered the house on that weekend in May 1961 I realised that it
was indeed a family home. Elizabeth's three sisters were being educated
there, her brother Philip being at boarding school. The family nanny was
still with them so once again I was very fortunate to find myself sur-
rounded with such help. Lady De L'Isle was devoted to her children. They
were all very important to her, and this little grand-daughter Shaunagh
was an added bonus. The staff also loved the children so it was indeed a
great privilege to be part of their lives.

We had several visits to Penshurst before the family left for Australia.
Shaunagh was three months old when we moved from London and made
our home there. The nurseries were on the first floor so our meals were
sent up in a noisy, rickety lift. Most of our time was centred in the nursery but it was the sort of house where the nursery door was always open
and where the parents, grandparents and other family members were in
and out whenever they had the opportunity.

I didn't have long walks alone as the village people were always stop-
ping me to ask how we were getting on and to admire the baby, often
inviting us in for a cup of tea. Many of them had worked at one time or
another in the house and Lady De L'Isle had always taken a keen interest

in them and their families.

Life was anything but lonely. Sometimes in the afternoon when the house was open, I would help for a while selling guide books or any of the attractive things on sale on the stall. Shaunagh would be sleeping in her pram nearby where I could keep an eye on her. We often had family friends with their children and nannies to stay and sometimes we would be invited out to friends for tea.

I had learnt to drive while I was with Timothy but his parents preferred that I didn't drive Timothy so I hadn't used my skills for five years, but now it was convenient for me to take Shaunagh out to visit friends. To make sure that I was competent behind the wheel the chauffeur took me out in a Mini and I soon remembered all I had to do and was given the go ahead to drive Shaunagh.

13   Life in a stately home

I loved Penshurst, with its wonderful Barons' Hall, left exactly as it had always been with a long gallery where the ladies would have walked on wet days, an armoury full of all sorts of weapons and armoury and the private apartments were full of portraits and beautiful furniture.

During these days, Oliver would go to London in the week, sometimes staying in their flat there where Elizabeth would join him if she wasn't needed in Penshurst. The time passed quickly and the day soon arrived when Shaunagh and I would be leaving for our three month stay in Australia. As Penshurst was closed for the winter months Elizabeth was able to visit her friends on her way to Australia but Oliver had to stay and work in the City.

It had been arranged that Shaunagh and I would go by sea so that Shaunagh could become acclimatised to the changing weather en route. We were taken to Tilbury one foggy day at the end of November. This was 1961. I couldn't believe the size of the SS Orcades, the P&O liner that was waiting for us. I had only been on a boat on the river Thames from Oxford to Abingdon before and couldn't imagine how this enormous ship could actually stay afloat! Needless to say that once on board I got lost several times before we got our bearings. We weren't actually travelling on our own as Shaunagh's godfather, a gentleman in his sixties, and his friend the seventy-eight year old Duke of Wellington were our travelling companions. We must have been a fairly incongruous group amongst the host of passengers, but it was fine.

When we were all at home Shaunagh's parents liked to have her downstairs with them after tea so that they could spend time with her. The Duke and godfather wanted to carry on this tradition on board ship. I would take her up on deck to them where they entertained her. I think that the Duke was quite used to handling his grandchildren but the godfather had only seen his godchildren at a distance so it was the Duke who organised the care of Shaunagh.

Often there was Scottish dancing or entertainment of some kind on deck at this time and Shaunagh would be urged to join in with the music. By the time I collected her, the three of them were all smiles and Shaunagh's arms were quite red from the handling of these two elderly gentlemen, but it was obviously a time of great enjoyment and it gave me a half-hour break.

I wasn't exactly idle during the journey as I had a friend in Thame who had thirty-five schoolchildren in her class. She had suggested that they might like to write to me. I had a great pile of their letters waiting for me at each port asking all sorts of questions, mainly on the changing weather conditions, the distance we were travelling, wondering what I did all day on the ship and whether I would see any kangaroos in Australia. One small boy was amazed that there were three swimming pools on the ship and another wanted to know what the captain's name was.

All these things kept me occupied while Shaunagh was sleeping or playing in her pram. Fortunately she was a particularly contented baby, which made life much easier. I was able to leave her in our cabin in the evenings while I had dinner as there was a baby-listening telephone installed. I would have been called if she had cried.

I wasn't brave enough to go ashore at the various ports of call. I didn't see the benefit of carrying an increasingly heavy baby around in the heat. There were several mothers in our part of the ship who wanted time off to explore a little so I could be seen with several babies in prams on the deck watching over them for an hour or two while their parents went ashore. There was plenty to see as people came and went and the children's letters to read if I had any spare time.

Disappointingly the ship's nursery couldn't accommodate babies so I wasn't able to leave Shaunagh at all. However I managed to enjoy several games of scrabble with friends I had made while Shaunagh slept beside me. It sounds as though she was always sleeping but I was able to keep to our old-fashioned nursery routine and she co-operated well proving that those now often out-dated methods worked well. The result was that we had a settled baby and a nanny who had a little time to relax. I have always found that a routine suited the children as they knew what was likely to happen next and it gave them confidence. It doesn't help a child to feel settled if sudden changes are sprung on them. Of course, the routine wasn't set in stone and sometimes changes had to be made.

We eventually arrived at Freemantle on the west coast of Australia on Christmas Eve, four weeks after leaving England. Most of the passengers were staying on the ship to tour around the coast of Australia over the Christmas period but it had been arranged for Shaunagh, me and our two gentlemen companions to leave the ship at the crack of dawn in a pilot boat, which took us ashore. We were taken to the airport for a flight to Melbourne where the Governor General's plane was waiting to take us on the final part of the journey to Government House in Canberra. Here Shaunagh was reunited with her parents and grandparents in time to hang up her stocking for her first Christmas.

This was all a great adventure for me. I had expected to be very much in awe of all that would await me in Canberra, but the family nanny had greeted us with enthusiasm and made life as easy as possible. Lady De L'Isle had wanted us to be part of the life of the house so we were invited down to lunch every day. We met the VIP guests who had been invited to Government House and I had the opportunity to speak to many interesting people. There could be twenty or more of us to lunch but Shaunagh and I would always have the chance to slip out early if the meal went on too long.

Much of our time was spent in the grounds of Government House where we enjoyed swimming in the pool, watching Lucy on her pony and just enjoying the gardens. We had occasional trips to Admiralty House in Sydney when the family accompanied the Governor General on one of his visits there.

On one occasion Lady De L'Isle told me that we were to have our lunch in the schoolroom. There was an important visitor expected for lunch who would be bringing staff with her, leaving no space in the dining room for us. This visitor was Queen Salote of Tonga. I had remembered the delight of the London crowds at Queen Elizabeth's coronation on seeing that Queen Salote's was the only carriage in the procession from Westminster Abbey to have its top open, despite the rain. The crowds cheered her enthusiastically all the way along the processional route.

Queen Salote duly arrived at Government House with her entourage. I had been told that she would like to see Shaunagh after lunch so we had a little while to prepare ourselves for the meeting. As Lord De L'Isle was the Queen's representative in Australia we were all expected to curtsey to him when we first met him in the mornings. I therefore knew how to do that but I now had to practice walking backwards so that I could leave the Queen in an appropriate manner.

The message came through that they were ready for us. I had dressed Shaunagh in her prettiest outfit, brushed her hair and made her look as good as I could. As we entered the room where the Queen was being entertained my nerves disappeared. She was sitting on a sofa, smiling her welcome to us, her hands out to take Shaunagh from me. She looked as though she was very familiar with babies. I duly walked out backwards and left them to get to know each other.

When I returned a while later I found a very sticky baby. The Queen had fed her coffee sugar crystals for much of the time that they had been together. Shaunagh had been delighted but I felt sure that the Queen must have been very sticky too.

14 Travels in Australia

Shaunagh's parents returned to the UK after Christmas leaving us in Australia to enjoy the next two months of sunshine. Early in March we flew home in a Comet airliner. In those days it was a thirty-six hour flight from Sydney to London, which seemed interminable to me. We were given one dinner on leaving Sydney, and another leaving Darwin. Throughout the flight we were reminded to put our watches back to lose the 12 hours difference in time so I wondered if we ever would get to breakfast time.

In the aeroplane Shaunagh was given a carrycot set on a shelf in front of my front row seat, where she was able to sit and wave to the passengers behind me. I fed her when I thought she was hungry as the clock was continually changing. At the times when I had a meal she liked to tear into pieces the thick table napkins that came on my tray. When she first needed a nappy change I took her to the toilet but the noise from the engines was so loud there that she was really frightened, so after that first time I changed her in her cot and all was well. We landed for about an hour at five different airports. We were able to leave the plane then and stretch our legs, which was a help.

While waiting for our luggage in the baggage hall at Heathrow one of our fellow passengers came up to us and told me that his heart had sunk when at Sydney he had seen that he was to sit on the plane just behind us, fearing he would have a very disturbed flight. He went on to say that he couldn't believe that hadn't heard Shaunagh cry once (he wasn't in the toilet when I changed her!) and congratulated us both. That was nice really. I knew that Shaunagh was a very good baby but liked to know that others appreciated her.

Back at Penshurst we picked up the routine of our nursery life and were soon caught up in the social events – tea with other nannies, children and their nannies coming to stay to be entertained and visits to Ireland.

Sadly, not long after our return, tragedy struck the family when Lady De L'Isle was diagnosed with breast cancer. She came to England for treatment but a short time after her return to Canberra she died. Penshurst was clouded in gloom as she had been much loved there. She had always had time for all she met whether they were friends or village folk and her presence was sorely missed.

When I first went to Penshurst she would ask when it would be convenient to come to the nursery to see Shaunagh. I had very quickly reassured her that I wasn't that sort of nanny and that she was very welcome at any time and we would love her to be part of Shaunagh's everyday routine, the more she came the better. After that she would drop in often, as did the rest of the family and Shaunagh had plenty of company at feed times and especially at bath time. In Australia Lady De L'Isle had been anxious to get to know Shaunagh again after the five months since they had moved to Canberra. So for me it was a real and personal sadness when she died. She was only in her forties then and had so much to look forward to in the lives of her children –no wonder her loss was difficult to accept. She was brought home and buried in the crypt of Penshurst Church and a while later had a very moving memorial service in St Margaret's Church, Westminster.

15 Days in Ireland

It was about this time that Elizabeth inherited an estate, called Lough Cutra, near Gort in County Galway in Ireland. It contained a ruined castle on the edge of a lake, much overgrown woodland, a couple of cottages and a stable block that had been converted into housing. I think the plan was that eventually the castle would be converted into a hotel.

To reach Lough Cutra I was asked to drive the family's Jaguar from Penshurst to Liverpool, 306 miles, with Shaunagh, the family luggage and three dogs. To cope with long journeys like this I used to have a series of small parcels in the car, which I gave to Shaunagh when she spotted a post van, a lorry, a coach, a petrol lorry or whatever caught her interest. Each parcel would contain something for her to do or to eat!

We had to get the dogs loaded on to the boat by 3.30 pm but weren't able to board as passengers until 8pm, so I had to find ways to keep Shaunagh happy till that time. While waiting to join the dogs and car on the boat I amused Shaunagh in Liverpool as much as I could, having a lengthy tea in a suitable coffee shop or hotel and occasionally passing an hour in a news cinema!

No one ever asked whether I would mind doing the driving or wondered if I was tired at the end of the journey. It was just taken as a matter of course that I would get on with whatever was expected of me and I honestly don't remember feeling any resentment that I was asked to do it all. I just accepted it as part of the job and my main concern was always that Shaunagh was coping well.

Once on board we settled down to a night on the boat before arriving in Ireland and driving a further 125 miles to Lough Cutra. On one occasion it was arranged for me to be met at Liverpool by friends of Elizabeth, who handed over their small child to come over to Ireland with us to have a holiday while her own nanny was away. This nanny was rather strict and very particular with the little girl in her charge so I was rather amused when it came to the time for the girls to settle down for the night. I sorted out the clothes they were to wear on the following morning from the hand luggage we had with us. There were no clean socks for our visitor to put on. 'Don't worry' said our small guest, 'Just turn them inside out like Nanny does'.

This same child became very grizzly on her second day in Ireland. I thought she was perhaps missing her home and family but I saw that I was quite wrong when she gradually produced a lovely measles rash! After several days of trying to keep her amused and at the same time making sure that Shaunagh was well occupied she began to recover. The next day Shaunagh came out in a rash so the tables were reversed.

Elizabeth and Oliver had plans to restore the castle and eventually open it as a hotel so we had several frequent holidays there. They were fairly eventful holidays as I was never quite sure what was going to face me. For instance on one occasion I ended up helping a very inexperienced American ex-soldier to do the sort of cooking that Elizabeth required. His main dish was eggs sunny side up, so dealing with devils on horseback or Boeuf Wellington, or even a simple roast chicken was a bit beyond him. It seemed to fall to me to help as and when I could.

I also had to cope with a very sweet but untrained pony that was suffering from laminitis and had to be discouraged from eating too much grass. I had no experience with horses so when I was needed to help Shaunagh to ride this pony it was very much a matter of the blind leading the blind.

The first task was to catch the pony and then, once saddled up and ready, it was a battle for Shaunagh to hang on to the reins as the pony put her head down to eat grass with Shaunagh sliding gently down her neck.

We had the added distraction of having a donkey in attendance, with all the bad behaviour of donkeys. Fortunately Elizabeth was more used to horses so could give us the help we needed.

Having the car in Ireland gave me a lot of freedom as I could take Shaunagh, and often other children who would be staying there with us, to find cowrie shells on the various beaches around the area and enjoy the odd trip into town. We did sometimes go into Galway with Elizabeth and would buy tweed or whatever was on offer and sample the delights of Ireland.

The local shopkeepers in Gort, our nearest small town, were delightful and always ready to welcome us, often with a drink while we were waiting to be served. They would sometimes suggest that Shaunagh could take down a dinky car from the sale rack and play with it in the shop – or even take it home till our next visit - but in a very nannyish way I had to dissuade them as I didn't want Shaunagh to think she could just help herself to whatever was on display when we returned to England!

On one visit to Ireland we were caught in heavy snow. The plan had been made for Shaunagh and me to travel home by car with her parents. The snow was thick as we drove from Lough Cutra to Dublin, where we were to stay for a night with the Guinness family at Leixlip Castle. I was glad we eventually arrived safely as the drive had taken much longer than usual.

Shaunagh and I were given a lovely room in the castle, which had a complete dinner service displayed around the walls. It seems strange that after all these years I remember little else of that visit. In the morning the snow had got heavier so it was decided that I should fly home to London with Shaunagh to avoid having a tricky and possibly long drive home from Holyhead to Penshurst.

Penshurst was completely snowed in so it was arranged that Shaunagh and I would go to Lord De L'Isle's London house, just a stone's throw from Marble Arch. The house had been shut up while he was in Australia so it was necessary for me to get the taxi driver from Heathrow to stop at a store to buy the essentials we needed, such as bread and milk and so on. Shaunagh was 19 months old at the time but fortunately was a very patient baby who managed to be co-operative in what could have been rather difficult circumstances, especially as it was quite late in the evening by the time we arrived and she must have been tired.

There was no cot in Lord De L'Isle's house, so for the first time, and in a strange house, she had to sleep in a full sized bed, which she did quite happily. When we were able to get back to Penshurst two days later, we found that visitors who had been staying there, who had also been delayed by the snow, were using Shaunagh's cot so I put her in a bed and she never returned to her own cot afterwards.

Sometimes it can be a problem to get a small child to change from cot to bed. One way I tried was to take the cot to pieces in front of the child so that it had gone from sight. The only real alternative then was to sleep in the bed, possibly with an added treat like special duvet covers. Half the success of such a move is to try to make the change when you think the child is actually mature enough to cope with it and is not having to make too many other changes at the same time.

16 Australia again

When Shaunagh was two we went out to Canberra again. Kate was Lord De L'Isle's second daughter. On her mother's death she had accompanied her father on his official duties acting as his hostess. She now wanted Elizabeth to relieve her for a few weeks while she had a break. At his time Elizabeth was in Hong Kong so we joined her there, spending three very hot days in Government House there before flying on to Australia. In Hong Kong we were given a room with a balcony. Our meals were served there so we were quite isolated. The gardens were lovely but I recall taking Shaunagh for walks in the nearby streets for a change of scene. She liked to watch the local school children when they were in the playground at break times. Once or twice we went into town to buy some dresses for Shaunagh. The dressmakers would produce beautifully smocked cotton dresses in next to no time so Elizabeth ordered several for us to take home.

The Chinese women would be sitting cross-legged on the pavements selling their wares. They seemed to be fascinated by Shaunagh with her chubby English look and would often go up to her and feel her arms. She wasn't too keen when that happened. I was just as fascinated by the seemingly petite Chinese children who shyly watched us from a safe distance. It was all part of being in a foreign country.

Once in Australia Shaunagh was considered to be old enough to accompany her grandfather and the family to Church. The routine was the same each week, although different churches were visited. Three Rolls

Royce cars would take us on our journey. Nannie Steadman, the family Nannie, in charge now of eight year old Lucy, the youngest of Lord De L'Isle's children, Shaunagh, and I would be in the last car. On arrival at the church, the clergy would be there to greet the party and would escort everyone into the church. The British national anthem would be played and the service would begin. Luckily we were about three rows back from Lord De L'Isle, his aides and the family so as long as Shaunagh was quiet all was well. I used to have a few small soft toys and a book to keep her occupied but don't remember having any problems apart from one time when I was praying and she wasn't. She had moved back underneath the pews to see what was going on behind us but came back when I called her. I don't think I ever had to groom her to behave. We expected the children to do what was more or less expected of them and on the whole they co-operated willingly enough. I was glad though when we all walked out behind grandpa knowing she hadn't let us down and I could look forward to lunch.

We were still invited to have lunch with the family and met many interesting people. I remember particularly the occasion when the Australian Prime Minister Sir Robert Menzies and his wife Dame Patty Menzies were there. We met to have a drink before lunch but when lunch was announced there was no sign of Shaunagh or Dame Patty. They were being tigers and went into the dining room on all fours to be discovered under the table!

I was able to have the use of a car at this time, which enabled me to take Shaunagh, Lucy and her nanny out and about a bit. On the occasions when we visited Lord De L'Isle's official residence in Sydney we enjoyed our jaunts to the shops and local places of interest.

After three months it was time to return to Penshurst. Shaunagh's parents had already gone home so we were travelling alone again on the long flight. Shaunagh was a star and no trouble at all during those long hours of the flight. It made life easier for me. She had a small case of her favourite books and games and when it was time to sleep I just got her into her nightclothes, read a story, and settled her to sleep, as we would have done at home.

Once home we fell back into our old routine. Shaunagh was developing into a confident little girl and enjoyed all that her life offered, especially having fun with other children who visited us quite often at Penshurst.

After another year, when she was now three years old, we found we were to go to Australia again. Aunt Kate had decided to get married in Canberra and wanted to have Shaunagh as one of her bridesmaids. Such excitement for Shaunagh! She had been a bridesmaid before but to go to Australia and take on the role again was something different. We flew out on our own as Elizabeth wasn't able to accompany us and Oliver had to keep his work going in the City. They were both to join us for the wedding.

When we reached Canberra Airport I could see Lord De L'Isle waiting to meet us, plus some press cameramen. The stewardess was at the top of the steps and seemed ready to help Shaunagh down so I let them go a pace or two ahead of me. I had reminded Shaunagh to curtsey to Grandpa. She was used to curtseying to him in Australia but on this occasion she was so pleased to see him that she began to run towards him for a hug. Remembering suddenly what I had said, she then stopped in her tracks to curtsey before continuing her run. It made a lovely sight on the television news that evening. She was wearing a white dress, white socks and red shoes and looked particularly sweet.

Once installed in Government House again wedding plans had to be made, dresses fitted, other bridesmaids and pages met, rehearsals gone through, all with the excitement of a big wedding. It made headlines in the Australian press and Shaunagh was featured in several magazines. The resulting newspaper accounts, which are now stained and a bit crumpled, are sitting in a large brown envelope amongst my memorabilia.

Sadly when the wedding day dawned it was raining, really a very wet day, which was so disappointing after the usual sunshine in Australia. It could have been in England. However we all made the best of it and I remember it as a very happy occasion. I was positioned in a small tent just outside the church but level with the altar so was conveniently placed when one or two of the smaller children needed a break to have their flowers rearranged, their faces wiped, their ribbons re-tied or whatever needed to be done. We got them all through without too much hassle. Shaunagh was very experienced as she had done it all before so was able to take it in her stride in her usual calm way.

After the excitement of the wedding, there was to be a children's party for the friends that were in the area. It was well organised but I had blown up a lot of balloons for the children to take home with them. The cars arrived, the front door was opened, and out went the children clutching their balloons but sadly it was a disaster. As the temperature changed from the house to the outdoors, the balloons all popped. So small children were driven home in tears and upset, which hadn't been my intention of course!

At the end of three months we were due to return to the UK, this time via New York as Elizabeth was there with friends. We had a twenty-four hour flight from Sydney to New York arriving quite early in the morning. I took a taxi to the flat where Elizabeth was staying.

Elizabeth said I could have time off to see New York while she looked after Shaunagh. I never seemed to be able to sleep on those long flights so I had gone for twenty-four hours without sleep. However as usual I did what was expected of me and followed instructions to go into New York City, feeling increasingly tired and feeling the weight of a necessary winter coat, heavy after the summer clothes I had been wearing for the past three months. However, I wanted to make the most of the opportunity to see the sights so went up and down Fifth Avenue, in and out of Macey's while drinking many cups of coffee to keep myself awake and even managed a visit to the Empire State building, returning in the early evening to the flat.

I was expecting to go with Elizabeth and Shaunagh on an evening flight to Shannon to spend the Easter break at Lough Cutra. I was surprised when Elizabeth said that she would take us to the airport saying that she would be staying on in New York. Shaunagh and I would be travelling on our own to Ireland. We caught the evening flight and arrived at Shannon to be met by the caretaker at about 8am. I had to admit that I wasn't looking forward to five days on an isolated estate on my own so I rang Shaunagh's father at his office in London and he suggested that I booked a flight home as soon as I could.

We left the following morning for Heathrow and eventually got to Penshurst and it was there that I heard the very sad and surprising news that Elizabeth had asked for a separation from her husband. To me they had always seemed very close but it seems that during the years since they moved to Penshurst things had gradually changed for them. Elizabeth had had to shoulder a lot of the responsibility of running Penshurst Place and once the house was closed to the public in October she was free to visit her friends all over the world. Meanwhile Oliver had to remain in the City to pursue his career as a young partner in his stockbroker's firm and just didn't have the freedom to be with his wife all the time.

Oliver had custody of Shaunagh with access for Elizabeth to see her as often as she could. We had to stay in Penshurst until Lord De L'Isle came home from Australia, then Shaunagh and I moved into one house in Chelsea with Oliver while Elizabeth moved into a house in the same area.

Eventually a divorce was arranged. I found that my role had suddenly changed and I was now a Nanny-housekeeper. I ran the house for Oliver, cooked and washed and entertained for him and Shaunagh. I found that I quite enjoyed my new role. We had someone in to do the cleaning while I arranged Shaunagh's routine, looked after Gussie the dog, entertained her friends and their nannies to tea and, among other activities, took her to dancing lessons with Madame Vacani. This was like going back in time as the children were taught not only dancing but also the finer points of making their curtsies and bows to their teacher and learning polite and civilised behaviour. I wouldn't say that Shaunagh was a budding ballet dancer, few of the children were, but they all seemed to enjoy the lessons and participating with their friends.

Once or twice a week Oliver would ask friends in to dinner and I would do my best to provide the meals he wanted. I wasn't an expert cook and once or twice met my match when I had to deal with pheasants and the like, but on the whole we managed well enough. His friends were very keen to chat to me in the kitchen while I was cooking and were always very appreciative so it wasn't the ordeal it might have been. We often went away at the weekends to stay in the country with Oliver's friends. That was a great time for me as Shaunagh and I would be entertained by the nanny of the house while Shaunagh played with the hosts' children. Nanny and I would keep each other company as we organised the children over the weekend.

At about this time, Oliver took Shaunagh and me to visit his half-sister, who was living in Blarney Castle. As I remember it, in those days in the sixties, it was a rather cold and bleak castle that had changed little over the years. The dining room was a long way from the kitchen. It seemed as if the food had to be brought along several dark corridors, so must have been difficult to keep hot. The resident pet wolfhound would scoop any cold meats that were left on the dresser. She could reach up that far with her tall legs and took advantage if the dining room was left unattended.

Of course, when I went there on my first visit, I was encouraged to kiss the famous Blarney stone. This meant climbing to the top of the tower and leaning backwards to kiss the stone on the far wall. It required quite an effort but was fun to do. I don't think I have been given the gift of being able to talk unrestrainedly as was the promise. I was amused to see an elderly Irishman positioned at the foot of the tower to collect any change that might have fallen from unsuspecting tourists' pockets!

17 Back to London

I didn't have much off duty time in those days but would sometimes take Shaunagh home to spend the weekend with my parents in Thame. They loved having her and even welcomed Gussie, a great character of a dog who made a big ploy of getting round my father, thus ensuring there was always a welcome there for her.

In London I was always free to ask any of my friends in to see me so I wasn't without company. One of my frequent visitors was Marie Byrne who remained a friend till the end of her life. I met her in Kent one weekend. Her employers were invited to stay with friends there so Marie and the three children that she looked after went with them. Oliver and I were also invited for the weekend with Shaunagh. Our hosts had three children with a rather inexperienced nanny who took one look at Marie and me with our charges and promptly retired to bed for the weekend with a migraine. So it was left to us to arrange activities for the seven children. It worked out well enough despite the eldest of our hosts' children, who seemed to do anything disruptive she could think of. Her favourite trick being to pull out the stoppers from the other children's armbands when they were in the swimming pool, a young lady to watch carefully!

By this time Shaunagh's mother had married again. She had a little boy called Maximillian. When he was just a few days old Shaunagh and I went over to Ireland. The maternity nurse had had to move on to her next baby so I took over for a week or two and looked after Maximillian, much to Shaunagh's delight. We went over on several occasions; the Irish girl who looked after him would have a holiday while we were there. Sometimes there would be an atmosphere in the house. At those times I would escape. I took Maximillian in his pram with Shaunagh and any other children we had staying there plus a picnic tea. It usually consisted of bacon and sausages, a frying pan, bread and butter and drinks. Not being a Girl Guide I took a firelighter with me to ensure that at least the food would be cooked. We made our way through the woods to a lovely open spot by the lake. The children would collect firewood, which we lit with a certain amount of excitement and I would produce the frying pan from the bottom of the pram. Once the food was eaten the children would then fill an empty Ribena bottle with water from the lake and spend ages dousing the fire before we left.

Maximillian would have a drink of fruit juice to keep him going until we all returned to the house. By then it would be time to feed Maximillian and bath the other children. With stories read it wasn't long before they were tucked up and asleep.

Sadly, Elizabeth's second marriage failed, she found it difficult to find any security and happiness and indeed married five times. She had another baby boy but after an unsettled time he was raised by the family of Lord De L'Isle's second wife and they lost contact with him. Elizabeth has settled now with her last husband living in Spain and has a much more secure life.

When Shaunagh was five she started to attend Lady Eden's school in Kensington, so much of my time was spent on school runs. She was a bright little girl and settled into school life well and we were soon caught up in the social whirl of tea parties, birthday parties and so on. We often saw her mother when she was in London but fortunately the situation wasn't at all traumatic for Shaunagh. She was settled in her life and accepted the circumstances of her parents, helped by the fact that we all did everything to give her security.

I was now able to meet with the nannies in the Park. We were often criticised as sitting around while the children played, discussing our employers, but in fact pretty much all our time was spent in discussing the children and exchanging tips on how to get over this or that problem. We were very much on our own in our nurseries so it was good to meet folk in similar circumstances.

Often on Sundays Oliver would invite one of his friends over for lunch. I would prepare the meal and put the oven on before we would all go to church together, usually to the Guard's Chapel or to the Royal Hospital in Chelsea. Shaunagh was always interested to see the Chelsea Pensioners in their colourful uniforms and particularly delighted if the Sergeant in charge reprimanded them for fidgeting if the sermon was longer than expected. I daresay it gave her a fellow feeling with them.

Sometimes we went over to Lough Cutra for a holiday together but at other times Shaunagh would fly over alone as an unaccompanied minor. I saw her off at Heathrow and her mother met her at Shannon airport. This gave me the chance to have a break, which I did enjoy but I was never resentful of the time I spent on duty with Shaunagh and her father, my main interest really was to make sure that she was happy and secure in her early years.

So much time is spent with the children that it becomes an essential part of a nanny's life to be there with them. You are gradually absorbed into the family circle. The parents are the backbone, the children your main interest, the other staff members are your fellow workers and even the dogs are part and parcel of it all. It seemed as though we were part of the same network that supported us all, not just then but actually for the rest of our lives.

When she was six years old Shaunagh and I arrived back at our Chelsea home after a trip to Ireland. We found a lady in the drawing room, who was introduced as Caroline. I was used to having Oliver's friends in the home as he had a large social group but I remember thinking that Caroline looked very much at home, sitting on the sofa, shoes discarded smoking a cigarette. We said 'Hello' before Shaunagh and I disappeared to the nursery to settle in again.

As I was unpacking Oliver came in to say that he had some news for us – he was going to marry Caroline. I asked when this would happen and I remember him saying 'a week next Wednesday and would I get Shaunagh used to the idea'. It had been over three years since we had left Penshurst so I quickly realised that things were going to change again for me.

I thought it would be best if I gave in my notice to Oliver. I didn't see why Caroline need inherit me as well as Shaunagh but she was adamant that I should stay as she wanted to have a family of her own so I looked forward to having more children to care for and was relieved that I could stay with the family for longer.

When I told Shaunagh that she was to have a stepmother, she said 'Oh good, I've always wondered what stepmothers were really like!' We prepared for the wedding day. Shaunagh was excited about the pretty dress that she was to wear, and the whole day went well.

We settled down to life together though I handed over the housekeeping to Caroline and became a nanny again in the true sense. The house in Chelsea was too small for all of us so Oliver and Caroline bought a larger house in Clapham Common. It had five floors with balconies on the first and third floors, running from house to house around a crescent. It worked out well for us all. I had the two top floors giving us a large nursery on one floor and bedrooms and bathrooms above. Luckily it had an excellent system of bells so that any of us could answer the front door or the telephone without going down all the stairs.

The routine went on much as before – I cooked and shopped and cared for Shaunagh but had a longer school run to get to Kensington and to see her friends. The parents joined us in the nursery for breakfast before school. Shaunagh and I would have our meals together in the nursery and Oliver and Caroline would come up to see us at bathtime and catch up with all the news. The only meal that Shaunagh and I had downstairs was Sunday lunch when there were usually visitors invited.

Quite often at weekends I would find myself driving, not to Liverpool for the trip to Ireland, but to Shropshire where Caroline's mother and stepfather had a gorgeous 16th century timber framed house, Pitchford Hall near Shrewsbury. I believe that when Queen Victoria stayed there as a teenage girl she wrote in her diary that it was 'a rather big cottage' but to most people it was a house of considerable size set in wooded grounds with a fast flowing stream running through the garden. It also had a natural pitch-well in the woods, a small lake on which the family manoeuvred coracles. The family had fun with the coracles, always tricky boats to manage but they coped well. The church in the grounds was the local parish church. One or two things were of special interest. One was a delightful tree house set in an ancient lime tree supported by stout props. It was thought to be the oldest tree house in the country, at least 300 years old, and records showed that the lime tree was 900 years old – more than double the expected life of a lime. It had been built in similar style to the main house, with a decorated ceiling. Shaunagh and visiting children were intrigued by it.

Shaunagh had a very grand bedroom, which could have alarmed a very sensitive child but in her usual level-headed way Shaunagh seemed happy to be there. In the wardrobe at one end of the room could be found a priests' escape tunnel that would have been used by Catholic priests hiding from Protestant priest-hunters. It went right under the house as far as the lake and made an excellent hiding place. King Charles I's nephew Prince Rupert was reported to have hidden there during the Civil War. There were many stories circulating about several different ghosts who had been seen but I have to admit that I always slept soundly and missed seeing them.

The Hall was looked after by a great couple, Mr and Mrs Rennison. They lived in a lodge at the main gate and had served at Pitchford for many years as butler and cook, working always to the very highest standards. We had wonderful meals served up by Mrs Rennison while Mr Rennison kept the house in immaculate condition. In the old kitchen there must have been 40 or more copper pans and saucepans, which he polished and shone to such a degree that they looked like silver. He would spend hours in his pantry working away to get the desired finish.

Mother and Father, 1927

Shirley, 1931

Shirley with parents, cousins, aunts and uncle

26 Wellington Street, Thame, Shirley's childhood home

Shirley with parents, sister Betty and husband Frank

David, 1951. Bottle in saucepan on gas ring

Philippa, 1952

Philippa with Nanny

Timothy's 4th birthday party.
Timothy far right with Nanny standing
behind him

Timothy, aged 7¼, with Nanny, 1960

Shaunagh, three days old, with her mother, 1961

Romaine, 1975

Rowena, 1973

Government House, Canberra

Lough Cutra Castle, 1961

Shaunagh at Penshurst, 1961

Penshurst Place

Above: Shaunagh with her father, step-mother and half-sisters, Romaine and Rowena at Pitchford Hall

Emma and Samina, 1988

The Brockie family, 1988

Marie, Christmas 1998

75

Joan and Shirley in New Zealand, 2006

Joan, 2005

Matthew

18 Romaine and Rowena

Life in London ticked on in routine as we got used to being together. In the centre of the crescent where we lived was a fair sized garden where Shaunagh could play with the neighbouring children on Saturday mornings.

After a year I was told the exciting news that Caroline was expecting a baby, so here was the family that I had always hoped for. We were all delighted when Romaine was born. It was truly exciting and so good to have a baby in the nursery again. Shaunagh, aged eight, was thrilled and was very interested in the new baby, helping wherever she could.

Romaine was a very serious little girl, born with a mass of dark hair and large eyes and an enquiring serious little face. As the months went past she showed that she was quite shy and when faced with strangers she would try to look back over my shoulder to avoid seeing them. She also hated any sharp noises and would react when the phone or doorbell startled her. I think she must have had sensitive hearing. One noise that particularly startled her was the cry of the peacocks if she was asleep in her pram at Pitchford and one of them decided to call a mate. It would take a little while to pacify her then.

She grew quickly and was the star of the nursery, much loved by us all. Caroline left her care to me most of the time as she wasn't at ease with small babies, but there was always Shaunagh there to play with her and to admire her.

There was one incident that tested my ability to cope with whatever might happen and which showed what a bright little girl Romaine was becoming. When she was about nineteen months old we drove back from Shropshire to London. There was no one at home when we got to the house, but as I got out of the car and lifted Romaine on to the pavement outside the house, the family's two Siamese cats came out to the car to join us. I was anxious to unload the luggage and get us all up to the nursery, so decided to put Romaine into her parents' bedroom, which was just inside the front door on the ground floor. I gave her the cats to keep her company and closed the door. When the car was unpacked and everything was upstairs I went back down to get Romaine – only to discover that she had turned the key and locked herself inside the bedroom. It was a very solid Victorian door that would have been difficult to push in as the screws holding it in place were old and long. She had actually taken the key out of the lock but nothing I put in would work the lock. Our neighbours had workmen in their house so I asked if they could help, but to no avail. They just stood in the hall with me pondering on the next step. No use looking for help from the windows as they had security bars in place.

All this time Romaine was quite oblivious to the rising panic I was feeling. She had taken the receiver off the phone base and was playing with that. I could see her through the keyhole and had been checking her as I passed the door.

I wondered if it was possible to get her to give me the key as there was a gap underneath the door. I talked to her for what seemed like an eternity asking her to bring me the key - then I had a brainwave. I slid a sheet of paper under the door and told her to put the key on the paper. After a few minutes she did just that. I pulled the paper towards me, the key sitting on it, and opened the door. The builders just couldn't believe that a small person of her age could have managed to understand what I wanted. She had the biggest hug in the world that day!

Within two years we heard that another baby was on the way, so there was more rejoicing in the nursery. Shaunagh was just about to go to Heathfield School in Ascot as a weekly boarder. In due course Rowena was born. She was different from Shaunagh and Romaine, but quite her own little person. She was born in hospital in London. After three days Caroline decided that Rowena should come home with us as she was crying in the nursery whenever Caroline saw her. The hospital staff were not very thrilled at the idea but let her come home all the same.

She was a very petite little baby with a very small frame and as the weeks went by developed well. She was very relaxed and smiley and less nervous than her big sister.

We were quite busy in the nursery now as Romaine had started to go to a Montessori nursery school in the mornings. She really hated going and would come home at 12 o'clock with a white face looking very drawn. I would give her a drink of glucose and tuck her up in bed for an hour until she had recovered enough to have her lunch. I was quite concerned for her and suggested that she wasn't ready for nursery school but her mother insisted that she should stick at it. She used to say 'Please don't open the car door and please let me come home with you!'

On the last day of the first week when I went in to collect her she was nowhere to be seen. The teacher told me that she had been sent to the kitchen because she didn't do as she was told. When this little white faced child was brought out to me I thought that I would never get her to go back into school on the Monday morning but to my surprise she went in like a lamb and didn't fuss again. So I was wrong, but Romaine nearly forty years later still says how she hated that teacher and remembering going to that school still makes her shudder.

There were another couple of occasions that come to mind when Romaine tested my composure. One was when she locked the back doors of her father's Volvo, which I used when out with the children. Locking the door was fine, she was 'helping me' she said. Unfortunately I had left the keys in the ignition as I wasn't ready to leave the car! I had to break the small window on the driver's door to retrieve the keys and consequently own up to Oliver when he came home from work. Romaine tells me that it was one of the times when I was very cross with her.

The other time was when Romaine managed to slip into the pond on

Clapham Common when we were out for our afternoon walk. The edges to the pond sloped and were moss-covered so it was an easy thing to have done. I should have been more careful, of course. In the event I put this damp little girl into Rowena's pram and pushed her quickly home while carrying Rowena in my arms. We were all particularly alert after that.

Rowena was very placid and grew into a very confident little girl. She spent a lot of time in the car as we drove the school run to take Romaine to school in Kensington. I would take her into Kensington Gardens to meet my friends before we picked Romaine up.

On our trips to Pitchford I would get the two younger children ready for bed, tuck them up in the car and leave London in the early evening so that they slept most of the way, only waking for me to carry them in to their bedrooms at Pitchford and settle down for the night.

19   London and Shropshire

Romaine and Rowena developed into two dear little girls even though their characters were so different. If there were visitors in the drawing room that they were to see, it was usually Rowena who would go in ahead of me. Romaine would follow rather reluctantly and not have much to say until she was comfortable with the strangers and could relax and be herself again.

Her mother was beginning to think that she was getting very disobedient but I was sure it had something to do with her ears. Perhaps she couldn't always hear what we were saying.

To test my theory I stood behind her one day saying 'Would you like some pink ice cream Romaine?' (Pink ice cream was her favourite at this time). There was no response to my query so her mother made the necessary arrangements for her to see a specialist who advised the use of tiny plastic tubes inserted into the eardrum, called grommets. This was a nuisance for her as it curtailed her swimming a lot and I think added her to her natural shyness.

At this time Romaine had quite a small appetite. To encourage her I used a divided vegetable dish, putting a few peas in one section, a potato in another and whatever meat or fish we had that day in another. She could then serve herself and was praised if she ate it all. Gradually I put in larger amounts of food, which she managed, and we were over the hurdle without making scenes about it.

In later years, Romaine and Rowena went to Wycombe Abbey School in High Wycombe. I used to take them out for lunch occasionally and they tucked into quite large helpings of pub food but still managed to take a bag of goodies back to school from the nearby supermarket, I would remember and wonder why I was so concerned for their seemingly small appetites when they were younger.

They were busy days in the nursery. I still prepared all the children's meals apart from Sunday lunch. We entertained their friends and of course went back to tea with them as well. Shaunagh came home most weekends and we quite often went up to Pitchford for a few days at half terms and holiday times and we all flourished. Romaine settled at her school and Rowena really enjoyed The Montessori School that Romaine had disliked so much.

One of our neighbours' older children had asked if Romaine and Rowena could join them on Saturday mornings as they were keen to set up their own 'Nursery School'. They had the girls for about two hours giving them craft work and lessons and songs to sing and letting them play in the central garden of the Crescent for a break. They were all quite serious about it and all ages seemed to thoroughly enjoy the activities and were keen to go each Saturday when we were in London. I imagine the older children gained a lot and certainly the younger ones didn't mind towing the line and doing what was expected of them.

20 Big changes

Life was easy and fulfilling. Here was a lovely family that I was happy to be part of, but suddenly I was aware of undertones in the house. When I returned from a day off the children would chatter about the things they had been doing but then would suddenly clam up and say 'Oh we weren't supposed to tell you that' or 'Mummy said not to do whatever it was when you were around' I began to feel uneasy and sometimes as we were leaving the house to go out Caroline would meet us and undo one of the girl's hair ribbons, or pull off a hair band or comment on their shiny shoes saying they looked very 'nannied'. As far as I could see it my work as a nanny was to see that the children were well turned out, at least when we left the house. If they got dirty when we were out that could soon be remedied, so I didn't quite understand the comments that I heard!

When you are part of the family life and working as a nanny you have to be always conscious of the fact that the children are not your children, that the parents must always take priority and that you should stand back where you can as much as possible. On the whole that has always worked well. I made a point of saying 'Ask Mummy or Daddy' to include them and did what I could. At the end of the day the nanny is the one who is there in the middle of the night, or when the children need comforting or are upset, or on long car drives. It was natural enough for the children to turn to you in confidence. At the end of the day though, if you don't work together in the interests of the children you are doing more harm that good by staying.

I had a lot to think about but I trod water for a little while. Then it became more obvious that Caroline would prefer to have the children cared for in a different way and that my days with them were ending.

Also, at this time, I had elderly parents who needed more of my attention. One day off a week and one weekend a month wasn't enough to see to their needs so very reluctantly I gave in my notice. There followed one of the most difficult times I have had in my working life. I had to keep going for the children's sakes. They and Oliver were quite upset. We were all upset, it was hard. They had relied on me for the everyday stability of the nursery and for the welfare of the day to day lives of the children. Oliver had the confidence to know that the children's lives had been managed well and suddenly it was going to change.

If my friend Marie hadn't come to collect me, I think I would have been driving round the ponds on Clapham Common for a long time before I would have been able to head out of London on the sad day that I finally left the family.

21   Stoke Mandeville

To be able to help my parents it was necessary for me to get a regular daily job and as a qualified nursery nurse I decided to apply for a post in the SCBU – the Special Care Baby Unit – at the Royal Buckinghamshire Hospital in Aylesbury. It was only nine miles from my parents' home in Thame. I needed two references. Oliver would give me one and I contacted Timothy's parents asking if they would provide the other, although I hadn't seen them for nearly 15 years.

When Timothy went off to his boarding school aged eight he wrote to me very often – I have some of his letters, including the one saying "Don't forget when I am eighteen I will look after you." but I had been discouraged from seeing him. On returning from my first visit to Australia I found a Christmas present from his parents waiting for me so I rang up to thank them and was invited to their Belgravia home for a drink.

It was a very strange occasion as every time I mentioned Timothy the subject was changed apart from one comment that he was very well. When it was time to leave I was invited back 'any term time' so it was quite clear that I had been put aside as part of Timothy's nursery years. The parents were very generous and through the years had regularly sent the chauffeur round with birthday and Christmas presents, which I duly acknowledged, but I had no further news of Timothy. I always wrote thank-yous but had no other contact with them.

Now I was asking for a reference. I was invited to go to their new home in Old Park Lane to see them and receive the reference from them.

I nervously rang the doorbell to be invited cordially into their flat only to find a twenty-three year old Timothy waiting to greet me. It was great to see him again but of course the years of separation made us seem more like strangers.

I was given an excellent reference and went on my way, not quite out of their lives at that point as I went back a couple of times to have lunch with them and once, when Timothy was forty-three, he invited me to his flat in London to have lunch with him. I wasn't sure what we would talk about but I needn't have worried as he spent the whole of the lunch asking me what we had done in the first eight years of his life. I haven't seen him since then, I am eighty now and he would be over sixty so perhaps our memories would have faded a little but it still feels as though he is someone special to me.

22 Elderly parents

B ut I had to get my act together and get on with the next phase of my life. I found a flat in Stoke Mandeville, part of the home of a retired nursing sister from the London Hospital. She was quite strict. There were several rules about how I looked after the flat and what the routines were but she was extremely kind and very welcoming. It was to be a very happy place for me especially as it was the first time in my life when I had somewhere to call my own home.

The work in SCBU was quite demanding, especially as I had never worked with a team of people before and of course I had a lot to learn about premature and sick babies. To begin with I found that I was working with the babies as they began to develop and were learning to bottle feed. As the weeks went by I was taught to tube feed and care for the smaller babies in their incubators, although of course the specially trained nursing staff were always in charge of them. Much of my time was spent with the mothers helping them to breast feed and care for their little ones and in assisting the doctors when we had the babies back for follow up appointments. Gradually over the years I built a place for myself there and became a member of the team in my own right.

We had one exciting event while I was working in SCBU. A mother came in to be delivered early as she was expecting triplets and was to have a Caesarean operation. The evening before her operation a scan showed that she was actually going to have four babies. The smallest baby was tucked away behind the other three – but there were definitely four baby spines. The staff were all on their toes as the time came for the operation to be performed, to much relief and delight when all four babies were delivered safely. And even more delight when it was found that all four were in good condition, weighing between two and three pounds each; two girls and two boys. One little boy needed oxygen for the first few hours, but after that was able to manage without it. All four were soon able to be fed and began to thrive. They were great celebrities for a while, of course, but their arrival in such good health gave us all the greatest satisfaction.

During this time I was pleased to be able to have some sort of social life that I could fit in around my shift work and I was able to give my parents the attention they needed. Marie would quite often come to stay in the flat, sometimes bringing the two little girls that she looked after. Our landlady was delighted to see the children there and specially pleased to have Marie's help in her garden. Also, I was able to have Romaine and Rowena to stay quite regularly for the weekend and often Shaunagh would join us from her school. I would drive to London to collect the girls from their school on Friday afternoons and the parents would come to pick them up after tea on Sunday. It was so good to be able to keep in close contact with the children and I dare say it was important for them to know that I hadn't actually disappeared from the face of the earth, because the bonds between us had been very strong.

It was more difficult to re-establish a relationship with Shaunagh. She had felt more let down than the younger girls when I left the family. I had been with her for almost 15 years and she resented my going. Gradually however the old bonds reasserted themselves and we were friends again, though on a different level. She sometimes came to dye her hair in my washbasin in Stoke Mandeville and made herself at home there. She liked to go to Thame with me to visit my parents, often going into the town to look for something in the charity shops. My father was appalled when she bought old 'Grandad' shirts home with her and admonished me for letting her have clothes 'that any old bod could have been wearing!' To him she was still one of the gentry, as he called them, and should have the best of everything. I think Shaunagh was quite amused.

I did think sometimes of the changes that her teenage years brought. When we went away when she was younger I would pack her suitcase with tissue paper between her clothes, all folded neatly. Now she was coming to see me with a canvas bag over her shoulder, her toothbrush and pants stuffed into her shoes, a book or two to read on the journey and space in the bag for her purchases from the charity shop.

Writing of suitcases reminds me of the time that Shaunagh and I were joining her parents and aunts and uncle in Paris. Lord De L'Isle was marrying again some years after his wife's death and we were all invited to Paris for the celebration. Shaunagh's Aunt Kate collected us from our house in Chelsea to drive to Heathrow. Shaunagh's case was strapped to the roof rack of their car but when we reached the airport we discovered that it was missing – fallen off somewhere en route to Heathrow.

We had no chance to retrace our steps as we would have missed our flight, so had to travel on minus Shaunagh's clothes. We had a scurry the next morning to get to the shops to find an outfit suitable for the occasion. As we were in France it didn't present too much of a problem. Elizabeth bought a very chic dress and jacket, which suited Shaunagh very well and if I remember, a few more clothes to replace those that were lost, so the visit ended happily.

After eight years my father became ill and died of cancer so I had more responsibility for my mother until her death at the age of ninety-two, two years later. She tried to be very independent despite failing eyesight. I went over two or three times a week taking casseroles and pies and puddings to keep her going. She had excellent neighbours who visited her all the time so she managed for nearly two years but as she became frailer she agreed to go into the local residential home. She knew the staff there, most of the other residents and many of the visitors, so it wasn't as traumatic for her as it could have been.

I often took her out in the car to make a change for her, which helped the days along. Six months afterwards, she died very suddenly just two days after her ninety-second birthday.

It was October, and as she had always loved trees Marie and I gathered all the vases we could find in the Baptist Chapel in Thame and soon the chapel was full of leaves for her service of thanksgiving. Many of her friends attended the service, a tribute to a very self-effacing lady who never wanted to be in the limelight but was always ready and willing to help in the background. She would also be missed as the expert with the Baptist's tea urn!

I feel eternally grateful for the way in which my sister Betty and I were brought up. We were given good standards that have lasted all our lives and were taught to make the most of what life brought us. Both parents must have made many sacrifices to send us to the Grammar School, buying our uniforms and the things we would have needed there, and giving us the benefit of a better education than they were able to have themselves.

Just three weeks after Mum died I had a letter from a housing association in Oxford. I had had my name on their list for a flat for a couple of years but here was a letter so soon after Mum's death to say that there was a flat available for me. So without any tears, I packed my bags and moved to Oxford, Marie coming with me as she wanted to share the flat. She had left the family she had worked with for many years and was doing temporary work so she needed the flat as a base until she was ready to retire.

We were often there together for several weeks at a time when Marie was in between posts and it worked out well for us. For the first time I had a full social life and I found some daily work that enabled me to have free evenings. I was fifty-five then and remember saying one evening 'We can go out tonight without asking anyone's permission'!

I had really stepped out in faith as I wasn't at all sure that anyone would want a fifty-five year old to care for their children but I had a nice surprise when I studied the local paper and saw that there were posts available and on further enquiry found that an older nanny was acceptable to many people.

My flat was situated just a stone's throw from the John Radcliffe

Hospital and I soon discovered that some married doctors there were looking for someone to care for their five month old baby – a little boy called Jonathan. He was very sweet and straightforward baby, which made life easy. Having worked for ten years with premature babies that had many problems before they could be handled normally it was a joy to be caring for a full term baby. It was so good to feed a baby who could devour a bottle of milk at the going rate.

Working as a daily nanny was very different from the years I had spent living in with children and their parents. Then I was on duty twenty-four hours a day with one day off a week and a weekend every month. Now I walked to where Jonathan's parents had a flat in the grounds of the John Radcliffe Hospital. The parents would then go into the hospital to work while I spent the day with the baby till one or other of them returned at about 6pm to take over.

Many child-rearing ways had changed during the years. But I had always potty-trained the children from a very early age. I would hold them over the potty after each bottle feed, with surprisingly good results even from a baby of just a few weeks old. As they got older I would pot them before and after meals, when we were going out, and when we came home again. It was just part of the nursery routine. By the time they were twelve months old Shaunagh, Romaine and Rowena were all out of nappies. Timothy was a bit longer but was dry by sixteen months. In the evenings I would lift them out of bed and sit them on a potty, very sleepily they would oblige, and were soon asleep again. It was never a hassle for them or for me. I also encouraged them to drink from a cup at seven or eight months old while still offering them a bottle at bedtimes if they needed it.

I had always been used to keeping my nurseries clean myself so now I found myself tidying the flat of my new employer, washing the clothes and doing whatever I saw was necessary so that when the parents returned at least the chores were done. I had plenty of time to do them while Jonathan was sleeping and there was still time for us to go out for a walk twice a day. Sadly for me, after a few months Jonathan's father took a step forward in his career and accepted a post in Cambridge so the family moved there. I was to discover that this was very much the pattern with the medical staff that I met and worked for. There were several changes in a couple of years as the posts were for a relatively short time.

For twenty months I took a post in North Oxford with a college chaplain and his wife who worked as an educational psychologist. Their little girl, Catherine, aged twenty months, was to be my charge and another baby was expected in a few months time. Catherine was a very energetic toddler and didn't mind being left with me when her parents went off to work on my arrival at their home. I found that she was still wearing nappies so my first task was to train her. She responded well as she was quite ready for that next step.

Previously she had resisted any idea of having an after-lunch nap but with a little coaxing and with the help of a story book, I persuaded her to settle in her pushchair and within a few minutes she was asleep. Her mother was surprised on her return later to find a lively little girl rather than the crosspatch she expected at the end of the day. Also, Catherine had made a great fuss over hair washing. She had lovely hair but it obviously needed more care. I decided to lay her on towels on the draining board in the kitchen. She was very secure there and felt safe. With the help of a few Smarties given at intervals we were able to have a shampoo. On my third day with her she was asking if she could have her hair washed again. After a week or two we managed it without the sweets!

She was such a bright and busy little girl, very determined but easy to channel. It wasn't that I was doing anything spectacular with her but I always expected a certain discipline and co-operation and usually found that children accepted that and responded. In six months, Catherine's brother Robert was born so my days were busier. However, after another year or so I began to want a change.

I had attended evening classes to learn to type so wondered if I would get some work using my new skills, but while I was considering that plan I was approached by the parents of Emma to see if I could look after her. Her parents worked as doctors at the John Radcliffe Hospital. Emma was five months old and not thriving very well. We were able to alter her feeding and she didn't look back. I had been with her for a month or two when her mother told me about a friend of hers who had a baby three months older than Emma called Samina.

This little girl seemed to have been causing her parents some concern. She cried a lot, didn't feed very well and was rather unsettled. The two mothers were keen for me to look after both babies and see if I could help Samina to become a happier little girl. I agreed to do what I could. It would mean that sometimes I would have Samina on her own, sometimes Emma on her own and part of the time I would have them both together.

The parents shared my salary, it seemed a good idea and certainly gave me more to do as I now tidied two flats and sorted two lots of washing etc. but had two very nice little girls to care for. Emma smiled her way through the days so I was able to give more time to Samina, who wasn't easy by any means but a challenge as I helped her along. Later we were to discover that she had a complicated syndrome that was perhaps the cause of some of her troubles. We had a double buggy so I was able to get out quite a bit, which suited Samina.

We were together for well over a year, both families moving into houses in the area before Emma's father accepted a post away so I was left with just Samina. She could be a wayward little girl. I remember one morning when she was nearly two; I arrived at her house to find her sitting on the stairs with her mother. She had been up for over two hours but refused to get dressed. Her mother was exasperated. I said 'Oh Samina, what are we going to do?' whereupon she went up to her room to get her clothes. She then gave them to me to help her to dress and in a couple of minutes was ready for the day. That was Samina!! In later years she went on to Reading University and now has a job in a library, which she much enjoys, and whenever I have seen her she has always had a very ready smile. She has done well.

When Emma and her parents moved away I needed to find another family to share with Samina as her mother only worked part-time and I needed to work every day. It so happened that as I was leaving the lovely church I attended in Old Marston I was stopped by a lady called Janet who asked me what I did for a living. She told me she was expecting her first baby and would be looking for help when she returned to work when her baby was five months old. She then asked me if I would consider looking after the baby. I liked her from the beginning and knew I would enjoy working for her. I introduced her to Samina's family and it was agreed that I should look after both children.

They lived quite near each other so it would work out well. There were a few weeks before Janet's baby would be born and a further five months before Janet would be ready to employ me, so I took a job in the meantime working as a cleaner in the Junior department of Headington Girl's School. This was an unusual move for me to make but it was fine as I was in close contact with the young children at the school. I was interested in all that they were doing and made to feel quite welcome there. It wasn't too onerous as I only worked there for one full day and one morning so I still had time to relax and enjoy my life.

During my time in Oxford I joined the Women's Institute (WI) and became programme secretary, arranging the monthly speakers. On one occasion the expected speaker rang at the last moment to cancel her visit. The president then asked me if I could talk to the members about my life as a nanny. With a certain amount of trepidation I did this, and to my surprise found it had gone down well and that our group had enjoyed my story. The neighbouring WI then asked me to speak to them and before I knew what was happening the county chairman invited me to an audition. If the representative members from thirty-five WIs in the county voted for me I would be included in the speaker's book so could be asked to speak anywhere. It seemed that they all thought I would be suitable so my name was soon passed around and I soon became expert at finding my way to all sorts of church halls and village halls in small villages in Oxfordshire. Soon I was being invited by other groups and became quite busy. On one occasion I was rung up by the chairman of a local University if the Third Age (U3A) group. I agreed to give my talk, but when I asked at the end of our call how many members would be in the audience, I was amazed when the answer was two hundred and fifty to three hundred: It was a combined group meeting. My usual audience was anything up to forty and I wondered how I could keep the attention of so many people, but somehow it worked well and as I was standing talking to them I remember saying to myself 'This is power, they are lapping up every word and no one has fallen asleep.'

Very often people would come up to me after my talk saying that I should write my story down – which is why we are here today.

With more free time I was able to go to the Thame Grammar School reunions, I did some charity work and often had coffee mornings in the flat. Marie was home quite a bit of the time to share activities and holidays so life ticked along quite serenely.

23 Oxford and the Brockie family

In due course, Janet had a little girl called Lucy, a lovely baby who was easy to care for and much admired by Samina, who was by then nearly three and getting quite independent. Inevitably, Samina's parents soon moved away to advance their careers. So Samina was replaced by two little girls, Tessa and Sophie aged two and four who lived in Headington. They adored Lucy and had much pleasure from helping her to learn to walk.

After a while Tessa and Sophie also moved away with their parents, but this worked out well as Lucy was soon to have a brother or sister. I was sixty then so thought perhaps it was time for me to semi-retire and just look after this one family. As Janet only worked three days a week it would be easier for me. They were really wonderful employers and always so appreciative of what I did in the normal course of my daily work. It was always a pleasure to go to look after their children.

In time another little girl was born, called Beth. Lucy was almost two then, so they were easily manageable. I still did the basic tidying in the house and the family washing and so on. I liked to do that as it encouraged the children to play on their own while I was busy. It wouldn't have been helpful to the parents if they had become used to being played with all day.

Lucy went first to a Mother and Toddler Group and then to the local playgroup so I was meeting a lot of mothers and children - but no nannies. This part of the social life I had known was now behind me, but

I adapted and enjoyed the company of those I was with. Sometimes I took my turn helping in the playgroup, which I enjoyed. As we went along, it was Beth's turn to go to the toddler group and playgroup and Lucy began to attend the local school. The children were very good at adapting to new circumstances and took each new phase in their strides.

In another two years Sam was born, Lucy was four and Beth two. Both were delighted with their baby brother. They greeted him in the hospital just an hour or so after he was born and were thrilled to hold him. Suddenly the house was a bit small for Janet and Andy and three children so they moved to a much larger bungalow closer to my flat, which was very convenient. I was by now even busier with extra rooms and three children to care for but there was always time to get things done and the parents always stressed that I should leave the chores if I wanted to, so I had no pressure.

Sam was again an easy little boy who tagged along with all the activities and school runs that were necessary with the girls. I used to put him in his pram in the garden to sleep after our first walk taking Lucy to school and Beth to playgroup. He slept there and was often still sleepy when it was time to collect Beth. After lunch he would play indoors while Beth had a rest and then we would go for a walk before meeting Lucy from school. It was such a happy household and we all thrived. Janet and Andy always had time for the children and it showed in their security.

I was thrilled to be asked to be a godmother to Sam, an added bonus for me.

Suddenly one day there was the surprising news that Janet was to have another baby– a bonus baby perhaps? The children were looking forward to the event, although when the day came for Janet to go to the hospital Sam was very disappointed to hear he had a little sister. He had two of those already and didn't want another - he wanted a brother. Once she was home, the new baby Kate was soon accepted by the girls but mostly ignored by Sam for the first few weeks. He pretended she wasn't there I think. But in a while he was as keen on her as her sisters were and she grew to be a treasured extra baby to the family.

For the first few weeks Kate didn't settle very well and was quite unhappy, for no particular reason. Often on the school run she would be crying in the pram. Sometimes I found I had to rock her in her baby seat with one foot while I was doing the ironing. Janet was quite sure that this was only a temporary phase and she was right. Gradually she became a smiley baby and was as happy as the rest had been, all her earlier grumbling forgotten.

Marie was at home more at this time so we went on holidays together and shared a lot of interests. She had come from Ireland when she was in her late teens and liked to spend a lot of time visiting friends and relations in Ireland.

My work kept me well occupied and content. As the children grew they had many interests and activities and were happy. They lived quite near University Meadows and a favourite game for them was to make a treasure trail. I would take the youngest child with me as we laid a trail of messages in the trees. I would only be a short way in front of them and as they read the messages and followed the directions I would be hanging small parcels on the final tree in the park. The parcels usually contained a pencil or rubber or notebook and a sweet or two, which they would find with squeals of delight no matter how often we played the same game! They were easy to entertain and very rarely bored because they had each other to play with. Occasionally one would be left out but I found another occupation for that one till they were altogether again.

I didn't drive the children at all. We were so near the bus stops that it wasn't necessary. We would sometimes take a ride on a bus for a change of scene in the holidays. They liked going to the local shopping centre, which took about thirty minutes by bus. Once there we would explore Woolworths, buy a small treat and then would have an ice cream or drink before leaving for home. Near the bus stop was a small playground that had to be investigated before we caught the bus home.

Once the children were old enough I took them to see the local pantomime in Oxford each year. First it was just Lucy then Beth joined us a couple of years later, then Sam and Kate. By this time the prices in Oxford had doubled so I took them all to see the Thame Players' pantomime. The repertory company there put on an excellent show, which we all enjoyed and could afford. The day ended with a visit to McDonald's for tea before I returned them home again

One day, out of the blue, I had a call from Timothy's mother asking me if I would be interested in taking part in the late John Peel's Saturday programme on Radio 4 called Home Truths. John wanted to interview an 'old nanny' and I was the only old nanny Timothy's mother knew. In due course a reporter came to Oxford to meet me, recording equipment in hand. She asked endless questions about my time as a nanny and then visited Janet and the children in their home asking them what it was like to be looked after by me. She also interviewed Shaunagh.

The result was quite a surprise to me. I was thinking that there were about two generation gaps between the children and me and had wondered if they looked on me as being 'old' and out of touch with their world. The children had no preparation time, but were interviewed and spoke just as they felt.

When asked what it was like to have me with them Lucy said 'She doesn't force you to do anything but then she's not a real softie either. She does things that are right but tries to make them nice for us at the same time' I was very touched.

Janet went on to say that 'I knew how to get the children to do what they should be doing'. When Shaunagh was interviewed she said that 'I had been her stability and rock' so looking back on all the years it seems as though I have done something right along the way. I count myself truly blessed and privileged to have been able to be part of the children's lives and of their parents, who always showed me so much kindness. Shaunagh and the other children are still a very great part of my life and I am sure they always will be. I couldn't imagine life without them. Our lives are intertwined and that network that I was part of is still there and as strong, if different, as it always had been. I am quite sure we will be part of each other's lives for always.

Some time after John Peel's interview, I came to the conclusion that

I should finally retire. For one thing I was approaching my seventieth birthday and getting more tired. The children could easily outrun me now. Also my friend Marie was becoming ill and I was needed at home to help her. Very reluctantly I told Janet and Andy that I must go. They only lived just down the road from my flat so I knew I would see them quite often. I explained that I would just leave the keys on the kitchen table and go home as usual as I hated the idea of leaving them all.

Janet rang me a week later to say that they had a leaving present for me and would I like to go in for a cup of tea. When I arrived the children were quite excited and wanted to give me my present straight away but were persuaded to wait till we had drunk our tea. At a nod from their mother they went to get my gift, a small cardboard box containing three CDs, the children explaining at great length why those particular ones were chosen. I was pleased to have them and thought to myself that now I must get the CD player I had been promising myself.

As we were talking, Andy walked into the sitting room asking casually if I had a CD player. When I said I was about to get one he said 'Don't worry, we have got one for you but we have left it outside. Would you like to come and get it, we're not very well organised today?' By this time the children were obviously excited. Kate was jumping up and down all the time and I was wondering what was going on as Andy and Janet were the most organised of people.

We all went into the garden, Andy opened the garage door and there inside was a brand new Citroen Saxo car – their CD player present to me. I was absolutely overcome, tears running everywhere. I couldn't believe that they should have thought of doing such a thing, let alone actually doing it. Granny came out of the annexe and said 'not more tears!' We all hugged each other before I could gather my wits and drive my beautiful car home.

It was a wonderful climax to my fifty-four years of working with other people's children, children who had given me so much love all through those years. If there was one lesson I learned through those years it was that nobody's possessions or position could possibly bring more happiness than I found in caring for those children. As I write my story in my eighty-first year and remember the days the children and I had together I feel content and glad that I chose a career that has given me so many blessings.

24 Marie

I had retired in the year 2000 just before my seventieth birthday with very mixed feelings. On the one hand I was looking forward to more time at home but on the other hand was aware that I would miss my working life and the companionship of children. But I really had no choice as circumstances were dictating what I should do.

At a coffee morning I met a nun who asked me what course I would be joining in my retirement. (In Oxford it seemed that almost everyone was electing to do further studying.) I remember thinking that I would surely find plenty to do in my retirement and twelve years later I look back and wonder where the time has gone. I have always had more than enough to fill my days.

My friend Marie, who had shared the flat with me for fifteen years, was showing signs of developing Alzheimer's disease. Her behaviour was becoming more and more erratic and I was increasingly worried about her. To begin with she just forgot everyday things, became muddled in her thinking and didn't seem to understand our normal routine life. She would question ordinary occurrences and would be unaware of what was going on around her.

I sought the help of our doctor who sent in a psychiatric nurse to see Marie who was most uncooperative during the visit. When she was asked what her telephone number was she replied 'I don't need my own number, I don't ring myself' and when asked her address the reply came 'I know where I live I don't need to tell you my address' and so it went on.

Things went from bad to worse when Marie began to disappear from the flat. Often I would have no idea where to look for her, so simply had to wait until she returned. On one occasion she had been to visit friends in Ascot. I went to Oxford station to meet her on her return but she wasn't on the train. No sign of her anywhere. Her friends said she had left their house a few hours earlier – where could I look for her? I rang the police but it was too early to consider her as a missing person, so I went home in case she rang me, that is if she could remember the phone number. After several increasingly anxious hours the telephone rang. It was a police station in Hampshire. Marie had taken a taxi in that area but the taxi driver didn't know the address she had given him so had eventually taken her to the police station. The officer dealing with her found my number in her handbag. So I then had to drive at midnight to Basingstoke, find the police station without any directions and no one about to ask, and console a very frightened friend. We were back in Oxford at 2.45am and I then had to then spend ages to settling her into bed.

The skills I had learned when looking after the children were much the same as I needed for Marie. If I said 'don't do that' she would become angry, but if I said 'let's do so and so' she would be more responsive. We had very difficult nights as she didn't sleep well but would be up and wandering round the flat trying to get out of the front door, which I kept locked with the key hidden. On one occasion she cut through the flex of our radio and would frequently pour milk into the automatic kettle if she wanted to make a cup of tea. This was disastrous as if I didn't notice what had happened and turned the kettle on the contents would boil up and spill everywhere. After the third new kettle I took to hiding it in a cupboard.

It would often take me an hour or two to get her settled into bed. I used to sleep in the bed next to her and stroke her hair to try to reassure her till she slept, only to have her wake again in an hour or so. She had endless restless energy; often we would walk for a mile or two but when we got home she would want to know when we were going for a walk.

She had relations and friends in Ireland who were concerned for her and would come to stay with us from time to time but they were unable to do more than that, although I always knew I had their moral support.

I knew this situation would have to come to an end for all our sakes but it was very difficult to find a suitable nursing home for her. I had a friend in Oxford who was the Chairman of the local Alzheimer's Society, who together with my vicar and other friends wrote to the local authorities eventually finding a lovely home not far from Oxford.

I went to visit the home taking with me a friend who had been the matron of a psychiatric hospital. I thought she would have an insight into the way that the home was run. We were shown around by the care manager and I was immediately impressed with her attitude and the ethos of the place. As we entered the reception area there was an elderly resident sitting on a chair with her coat on. The manager asked her where she wanted to go – the answer came 'To Liverpool' – we were in Buckinghamshire. Without blinking an eye the manager looked at her watch and told her that she had just missed the bus to Liverpool but there would be another one tomorrow. She added that we were just about to have a cup of tea so if this lady would like to join us she would be very welcome. It was such a simple approach, no one had criticised the old lady or made her feel in any way that she was confused and peace was maintained as she looked forward to going to Liverpool the following day.

Later on, we were shown a relaxing room where residents were taken if they needed to calm down. Fibre-optic lights had been installed there, soft music was being played and comfortable chairs placed all around. As we were looking at everything the door opened and an elderly man came in. My friend, a strict disciplinarian, tried to usher him out of the room saying we were busy, but the manager quietly took over and showed him the lights and how they worked, just talking to him quietly and we all left the room together. I knew without a doubt that Marie would benefit from being there.

Marie had always been a very independent person – a true Irish free spirit- and had always made her own decisions, so it was very hard for me to make all the arrangements for her future care without her knowledge. She had to give her consent to go into the home. This consent caused us a few nightmares and had been difficult to obtain. When her social worker came to see us with the form and explained it to Marie she blankly refused to sign it, saying she had a home and didn't intend to find another one! The form was left with me to see what I could do. I had little success until one day, after she had been particularly difficult, she recognised that I was upset so asked me what she could do to make me feel better. I quietly said 'Will you sign your name on the form?' to my relief she did just that. Imagine my consternation when the social worker returned and said she didn't know whether she could accept the signature as Marie probably didn't know what she had been signing. At that moment I think I was about to explode but managed somehow to contain myself. Perhaps the social worker could read my body language, or just saw sense, but for whatever reason she changed her mind and the form was accepted.

It was a very hard day when I had to take her to the nursing home. Marie was saying she would only stay there for a day or two so there was no need to unpack her case! I was very upset to leave her there and drove home in floods of tears but it turned out to be the best thing that could have possibly happened to her. She was completely free there to do whatever she liked, walk round at night, go to bed in the day or whatever she fancied. There was no one to say 'No' to her, just very patient and kind people who persuaded her to do what they wanted. I realised I had been exasperating her at home by having so many restrictions, however necessary they were – not to go out of the front door, not to make jam sandwiches with the whole loaf of bread at 3am, not to pour water into the coffee granule jar, and so on.

Marie settled down well after one or two hiccups in the first week or two. I visited her three or four times a week to begin with and then more often as her condition deteriorated. I went in most days to help her with her lunch. I got to know the other people there, both staff and residents, we were quite a close community who supported each other as we supported our loved ones. I don't think Marie could have given me a name but she always recognised me as being familiar. She was always very pleased to see her Irish folk when they came to stay with me. On hearing the Irish accent she would sometimes give me a puzzled look and say 'You can go now' so I knew where I stood for that moment.

Two and a half years later Marie died. She had fallen out of bed and broken her hip. Inevitably she developed pneumonia and died three weeks later. She had been a very close and dear friend but I felt we had done the best we could for her under such difficult circumstances.

Throughout this time I was being supported by some ladies I had met from my church in Marston. They had formed a Friday morning bible study and prayer group. We met each week during term time. For the first few years we met in one house and were always led by the same friend. Then changes took place and we would meet in each other's homes and take it in turn to lead the morning studies. We developed into a band of very firm friends, we could trust each other with any problems that we were facing and could discuss them in confidence. This meant that they were all there for me while I was dealing with Marie's illness and were on hand to give help and advice. It was an enormous help to be able to share with them.

I carried on seeing Shaunagh and Romaine and Rowena. Shaunagh married when she was very young. The wedding took place at Pitchford Hall in Shropshire, her stepmother's family home. I was there to help her get dressed and to be part of the proceedings. The young couple had a house in London. When the first baby, Elizabeth, was born I went up to give Shaunagh a hand in the first few days, and again a couple of years later when Harry was born. It was great to be involved with the second generation. Sadly, after ten years, Shaunagh and her husband were divorced, but a few years down the line I heard that there was to be a second wedding when Shaunagh would marry Crispin. This time it was quite a different occasion, to be held in Brixton in London. We all piled into a Range Rover and drove to the Registry Office where the wedding took place. Quite a lot of giggling went on with Elizabeth, now a teenager, and Harry and Crispin's three delightful children, it was a very happy time and we all enjoyed the rather relaxed day.

Later Rowena married James at Pitchford. She had converted a barn into a most attractive home on the Pitchford estate and was married from there. I stayed overnight and went to bed earlier than most of the guests leaving them to the delights of the disco as I had to leave early in the morning to visit Marie. As I was going to collect my car, parked in a cornfield, I was amused and surprised to see Rowena and James emerging from a caravan, pillows in hand, en route to find a bathroom in the house.

Rowena now has two little girls, Georgiana and Serena, to add to my 'family.' It's a real pleasure when they go out of their way to call on me so that I can see the children. To that generation I am known as Nanny Smith to differentiate between other nannies that they know.

25 Meeting Joan and coping with cancer

About a year before Marie died I was introduced to Joan, not realising that meeting her would change many things in my life. She is an ordained minister in the Church of England, retired but with permission to officiate in the Salisbury diocese. She lives in Baydon, a village near Marlborough in Wiltshire.

In her early retirement she had decided to study for a human biology degree at Brookes University in Oxford. To do this she needed to find accommodation somewhere in Oxford during the week as it would have been difficult for her to travel up every day. For the first year she stayed with a friend of mine, Clemency. When Clemency wanted to go on holiday she asked me if I could have Joan to stay for two weeks.

I had never had a Reverend to stay before and was a bit apprehensive – would she be very straight-laced, would my small flat be big enough or smart enough, etc. etc.? I need not have worried, as soon as Joan came into the flat I was sure we would get on together. She was so easy and not the least bit straight-laced.

When staying with Clemency she had been used to getting her own supper when she came home from Brookes and then sitting in her room to study. In my flat I was usually about to have something to eat at the time she got home so suggested that she might like to come in and share the table with me. We soon became friends and I learned that she was quite happy to sit with me and chat or watch television in the evenings until the pressure of work drew her back to her studies.

At the end of the two weeks she returned to Clemency's house but we missed our companionship. She took to coming to have supper with me every Wednesday, which we both enjoyed.

When Marie died, Clemency came to me to ask if there was anything she could do for me. I replied that I would like to have Joan to stay all the time. That was good for Clemency as she had then decided to sell her house and Joan would have had to find new accommodation somewhere else anyway. Was my guardian angel at work again?

We settled down into a pleasant way of life. Joan worked very hard at her studies and if she had time off in the day because of evening lectures she would come home and have a nap on my sofa. She had a heart condition that caused her some problems and needed to have extra rest.

Sometimes, at the weekend I would go home with her. I was then able to meet her son and daughter when they visited her and also to be with her when she was taking services in one of the six churches in the benefice. That was a treat as she is an excellent preacher and I always enjoy her sermons. She only took two services a month as so much of her time was taken up with her university work. Brookes is an excellent university and the work was very intensive and demanding.

Joan has one son, Richard, in New Zealand, another son, Christopher in Guildford and a daughter Rachel living north of Cirencester. Chris and Rachel are particularly close and keep in touch every day, not so easy for Richard in New Zealand. I thought that they might find me a nuisance as I turned up at their home so often but they welcomed me and soon became used to having me around and made me feel like one of the family.

It was at about this time that I joined some friends for a brief training session that enabled us to become invigilators at Brookes University. We would be invited to invigilate several times a week during the examination periods. It was very interesting. I was put to work with the students who had special needs of one sort or another. Some would have partial sight or partial hearing, some had physical conditions that made studying difficult for them and many were dyslexic.

These students were given a great deal of help by Brookes and given every opportunity to study along with the rest of the students. They were given more time to write their papers and were in smaller groups, occasionally sitting in a room on their own if that helped them. Once or twice I was asked to write the papers at the student's dictation. This was very tricky. I had to write quickly and legibly remembering everything that was being said but not interrupting to ask a student to repeat something I had forgotten or missed. I was glad I didn't have to do it too often. Later Joan joined me and we would work the same sessions but not always with the same group of students.

A few months after Joan came to stay with me, I was driving along an Oxford street on a clear night in the semi-darkness wondering why all the other car drivers were using fog lights. When I parked my car I saw that the other drivers only had normal headlights on - I was seeing double. I made an appointment the following day with my optician and discovered that I had a macular hole in one eye. This felt a bit worrying as my sister, Betty, suffered from macular degeneration and I thought the two conditions could be similar. However, the consultant I saw at the eye hospital assured me that he could operate to close the hole.

I went to the hospital on the appointed day feeling quite optimistic about the outcome. The operation was a test of my ability to keep still as it was carried out with an injection into the eye while I was fully awake. I was told to keep absolutely still for the forty-five minutes that the operation took. I managed to do that but found afterwards that I couldn't stop shaking. I suppose some sort of shock had set in. Fortunately a very patient Joan was with me and was at home during the next two weeks as I was required to lie flat on my front for fifty minutes out of every hour for that fortnight. Joan looked after me but I know she was pretty frustrated when I got up during my fifty minutes to talk to friends on the phone or to get a drink. I insisted that I would hold my head down, but she wasn't satisfied.

I found out later that my surgeon had abandoned that plan with all his subsequent patients as he thought it was no longer necessary!

On my return to the hospital for a follow-up I was told that the operation hadn't been successful and I would have to have it done again, with a different procedure. A few weeks later I went in again, this time without having to lie face down for a fortnight afterwards, so didn't need so much help at home. At my follow-up appointment I was shown a photograph of the surgery and was able to admire the surgeon's handiwork, which was most impressive. 'That was a good piece of sewing' said the surgeon 'It is a pity that it hasn't worked.' The trouble was that I still had no central vision as the second operation hadn't helped. I still have enough peripheral vision to enable me to drive, but I still see double – a condition that you gradually adapt to and accept.

One day Joan asked me if I would go to New Zealand with her for three months, staying in youth hostels and finding our own way around. I don't think I took too much time to consider the plan as I had every confidence that Joan knew what she was doing. She had been on a backpacking holiday to Australia and New Zealand on her own a few years earlier.

It was an exciting time as we made our plans with the enormous help of Joan's son Chris. He enjoys making travel arrangements and amazingly was able to find some air miles to help us on our way. I had travelled with the children in my nanny days but then the details had been worked out for me, so all I had to do was to pack, look after the children and be ready at the appointed time. In a way this was much the same as I just listened to everything that was being planned by Chris and Joan.

But there was a snag: A few months before we were to go on our travels I noticed something worrying when I was having a shower. I said nothing to Joan but made an appointment to see my GP the following morning, a Friday. I had a Bible study meeting to go to first, which usually ended in coffee at 11 o'clock. I made my excuses and went off to the surgery. The doctor examined me and told me that he was 99.9% sure that I had breast cancer.

Somehow I couldn't go back to my flat, so I drove to the Tesco supermarket just outside Oxford. I knew that Joan stopped there after lunch on Fridays on her way home. I waited until I saw her at the vegetable counter and told her my news. (I dreaded that vegetable counter in the week or two afterwards.)

We went off to have a cup of coffee in the café and talked about it all. I was then able to cope and went back home having off-loaded my news onto Joan. It seemed easier after that to tell other people. Telling my family was more difficult though as my nephew Stuart had lost his wife to breast cancer earlier that year.

I was really blessed as I was referred to a wonderful cancer surgeon at the John Radcliffe Hospital within two weeks. Joan came with me to the appointment with the consultant. She was studying the molecular aspects of cancer as part of her university course so was quite knowledgeable about the condition. The consultant went through the details of the treatment I would have after surgery saying that radiotherapy would be followed by hormone treatment. Joan then asked if it would be possible for me to be given chemotherapy. We were told that chemotherapy wasn't usually given to patients over seventy-five, which was my age. But the consultant was such a caring doctor. She looked at us, listened to what we were saying about how active I was and that I had no other health problems, no heart trouble, no blood pressure problems, no diabetes, and so on, and then quietly went on to say that she would put me forward for chemotherapy if the consultant oncologist agreed. How can you criticise the NHS when you receive that sort of treatment? It made such a difference to know that I was being treated as a person rather than just another in a line of patients.

Within three months I went into the Jane Ashley Breast Cancer Unit at the Churchill Hospital in Oxford. It was a ward that had been set up as a trust in memory of Jane Ashley who had died of breast cancer. The ward was only open from Monday to Friday and it was run by the nurses. There was a kitchen that both the patients and their visitors could use, with a fridge and microwave. Any food could be kept there and used when needed. There only seemed to one rule – that all dishes and cups should be left on a tray so that the staff could put them in the dishwasher at the end of each day.

Joan came in with me on that first day and sat to wait till I returned from the operating theatre, doing her study work to pass the time. The operation was quite successful and apart from a few problems with low blood pressure I was soon on the way to recovery.

There were only about twelve patients in the ward. I had a side room, which was useful as I seemed to have a lot of friends visiting me and what seemed like endless telephone calls as my sister and friends rang to enquire about me. The phone was always brought into me in my room, which gave me the chance to chat. Shaunagh was still very much a part of my life and was constantly caring about what was happening and telephoning from her home in Spain.

We all used a sitting room at the end of the ward that had been set up with comfortable armchairs, a television and plenty of books and games to keep us all amused. There was a large wooden table in this room. At breakfast time it was laid with plates and bowls and cups and saucers with cereals, marmalades and jams put out on the dresser, together with a kettle and toaster. We were all free to go and help ourselves to whatever we felt like and at what time suited us. It was home from home indeed. More reason to congratulate the NHS. It made a huge difference to our recovery I am sure.

Joan collected me on the Friday, only five days after my operation, and made sure that I rested and followed doctor's orders.

The chemotherapy treatment wasn't much fun as I felt drained of energy after each session and was just beginning to recover when it would be time to go back for another appointment. There were five sessions in all, at three weekly intervals. I had a couple of weeks break and then had fifteen radiotherapy treatments, three a week. They didn't bother me at all, though it was disconcerting to find my skin had been burned off!

The chemotherapy had caused my hair to fall out so I went off to Banbury where I could purchase a wig. It was a traumatic day as I was exhausted by the whole effort of driving there and having to make a decision about which one suited me, how grey should it be, and so on.

In the end I was so tired and fed up by it all that I chose one that seemed reasonable and hoped for the best. Amazingly it turned out to be really very flattering, better than any hairstyle I had ever had. Once my hair was really thin I decided that I should have the last of it removed. Imagine me sitting on a chair while Joan shaved my head. What sort of friend could you ask to do something like that for you?

We had fun times with this wig though. Once I was walking with Joan along the path near my flat when the wig caught on a holly bush and was lying on the path in front of me. You can either laugh or cry. We laughed as I tried to put it back on the right way round without a mirror. On another occasion we were in Stratford-on-Avon, staying in a youth hostel there for me to see what these hostels were like. We took ourselves onto the top deck of a double-decker sightseeing bus where, of course, my wig threatened to blow off. I had to sit there holding it on, trying to look inconspicuous. Then on a third occasion we were on a boat going over to Swanage. It was naturally very windy and difficult for me to keep the wig on. Joan said 'Just take it off, no one will notice!' I did just that, feeling very odd as we walked past the other passengers with my quite bald head and was mortified when Joan suggested that we moved to another part of the ship to get out of the wind. Once there we found it was even windier and in returning to our original seat I had to pass everyone again. To be honest I don't think anyone noticed.

I was soon on my way back to my usual occupations and found that all sorts of people were asking me to talk to someone that they knew who was going through the same thing and wanted some first-hand information about it all, so I was able to share my experiences.

Although I had coped very well with everything that had come my way since I discovered I had cancer I was very uptight about having to wear a prosthesis. I just couldn't bear the look or feel of it and I was getting paranoid about it. I decided to go back to see my Surgeon and explain how I felt. She was so understanding, saying she was looking at me holistically, and if I felt so strongly about it all she would consent to giving me a second operation when I returned from New Zealand

and remove the other breast. I was very thankful and appreciative of her attitude. Once again I felt I was being treated as a person rather than simply a patient.

26 Backpacking in New Zealand

Now came the time to think seriously about our trip to New Zealand again We were each taking a small case and a backpack so had to decide what clothes and extras we needed to have, and what we needed to leave behind. Shaunagh had invited me to have lunch with her in London, always such a good opportunity for us to be together again and to go with her to unusual restaurants. On this occasion we were in Victoria and after lunch we went to a nearby sports shop where Shaunagh bought me several small soft plastic bags. They had net tops to them and were designed so that you could pack your different items and see at a glance what was where. One for socks, one for T-shirts, one for undies and so on. They were a boon and made the whole packing business much simpler and more organised. Quite a laugh to find Shaunagh organising me instead of the other way round. The tables were turning and our roles beginning to reverse.

Joan and I were taking the minimum of everything but had to make room for notebooks, as we would be keeping diaries of our journey, our cameras and the inevitable chargers for them and for our mobile phones. We also had to find the space to include plastic plates, cups, knifes, forks and spoons, as we would be self-catering in the youth hostels. Saucepans would be provided for us.

Packing done, farewells said to friends and families, we were ready for the off. Christopher drove us to Heathrow and went with us to the check- in desk. We made for the one that had our flight details on but

Christopher said 'Go the next desk, you won't have to wait so long' To our amazement we discovered then that he had upgraded us to first class. I couldn't believe it. Once on board the plane, our goodbyes said to Christopher, we were made very comfortable for the long flight. We had beds, pillows, blankets and even pairs of pyjamas and slippers and a spongebag that contained all the cosmetics we would be likely to need. Such luxury. The cabin crew were on hand to see to our every need. As well as the meals that were provided we could have any other food prepared for us and a great selection of drinks.

Our own television screen was in front of each bed so we were able to watch a film if we weren't sleepy. This was the way to travel! I couldn't help wondering what my parents would have thought of it all. I was sorry to think that they didn't know how specially blessed I was to have met Joan and her family.

We stopped off in Sydney for a couple of days before going on to New Zealand to begin our adventures there. We went firstly to North Island where we hired a car for the length of our stay. Joan found a car hire firm who would rent out basic Japanese cars for £8 a day. This was an economical option and enabled us to visit out of way places as well as the more popular tourist areas. Joan took over the driving as she was used to an automatic car. I did have one try to master the system but wasn't encouraged to repeat the effort, so I had the joy of being driven everywhere.

New Zealand is a wonderful country with breathtaking views at every twist to the road. As Joan and I went round yet another tight corner we would say 'Just look at that!' There were so few cars on the road that we would pull into a suitable passing place if another car came along behind us, we became used to having the road to ourselves. On one part of our journey we drove for something like eighty kilometres and didn't have a single car pass us.

The Youth Hostel Association (YHA) has a great network in New Zealand and the tourist information centres are excellent. We were able to find out the information we needed at every place we reached and booked ourselves on all the tours that interested us. We took these tours so that Joan wasn't driving more than was necessary. We used the car mainly to get from one area to another. The YHA or tourist information centres routinely arranged for a shuttle bus to pick us up from our hostel to take us to the departure points for the tours, which made life easy.

We travelled from the northern most point of North Island to the southern most point of South Island, including Stewart Island. The New Zealanders were very proud of their beautiful country and very knowledgeable about the flora and fauna, so had much of interest to share with us all. We visited Maori settlements, ate a dinner cooked in the traditional Maori way, visited their museums and learned to appreciate their history.

There was so much to see and so many new experiences to enjoy. On one occasion we went out on a whale watching trip. I had seen many documentaries about whales but nothing compared with the utter joy of watching a whale bring up its enormous tail and make a dive just in front of your boat. I found it a mind-boggling sight and very moving. It was made even more memorable by seeing a royal albatross leave the spot where it had been floating on the water and take flight just as the whale disappeared under the sea. It was truly a huge bird with its nine foot wing span. While all this was happening about sixty dolphins decided to play around and under the boat, leaping out of the water all the time. The captain put on the loudspeaker so that they could hear music. It made them jump even higher it seemed.

Another time we watched tiny eighteen inch penguins come back to land after a day's fishing, their bellies swollen with the fish that they were bringing ashore to feed their waiting chicks.

We also had a flight in a helicopter to the top of Mount Cook. We landed in the snow nearby and had the opportunity to take in the spectacular scenery before being taken back to our starting point.

One time when we were staying with Joan's son Richard he took us on a trip to Queenstown. He was determined that we should enjoy some of the challenges that New Zealand had to offer so he took us up one mountain on a gondola. Once up to the top station we had no choice but to go on a chair lift to take us farther up the mountainside before coming back down in a luge, travelling quite fast, lying prone and keeping all our fingers crossed hoping we would have a reasonably soft landing. Richard introduced me to one of his friends as 'the 75 year old who came down the luge at 75 miles an hour.' And so the stories could go on.

While we were in South Island we were able to have a very exciting trip on Milford Sound in a boat that had overnight accommodation. We were taken through an enormous gap between rock-covered mountainsides and saw many waterfalls wherever we looked; it was a majestic place in the darkening skies. After settling into our luxurious cabin we were taken on some smaller craft out into the waters of the sound, at least I was in a smaller craft but Joan was more adventurously using a kayak. It was a mysterious place and very awe-inspiring. After a delicious dinner back on the boat we all went on deck to see the night sky. There the Captain asked us all to stop talking, to turn off our mobile phones and to stand quite still. He then turned off the engines and machinery of the boat so we could experience the absolute quiet of New Zealand – as he told us that was how New Zealand would have sounded to the first settlers. Magic.

It rained hard overnight so that on our return journey the following morning the waterfalls were much larger than the night before, it seemed as though the mountainside was just emptying itself of all the rain.

Our travels took us to Christchurch on a couple of occasions. We spent quite a lot of time in the Cathedral there and in Cathedral Square. Sad now to recall that much of that area has been devastated by the earthquake in 2011 that virtually destroyed that beautiful Cathedral.

Too soon it was time for us to hand in the car and return to England. I had felt quite cut-off from all that had been happening at home so knew it would be strange to pick up the life in Oxford that I had been used to. How would I settle down after all the stimulation and excitement that we had experienced?

No sooner were we home again, our cases unpacked and our washing up to date, when I had a phone call from the lovely breast care nurse who had been looking after me. She suggested that I might like to go into the Jane Ashley Unit in ten days time to have my second operation, so here we go again.

This time I felt a bit like a fraud as I didn't actually have cancer anymore. As I joined the other ladies in the ward I was very aware of their worries, while I was going to have a straightforward procedure with no chemotherapy or radiotherapy, yet still a fairly drastic operation. I recovered quite quickly, just the usual problem of low blood pressure afterwards. I was becoming used to that as it always seemed to follow an anaesthetic for me.

27 Life in Baydon

At about this time Shaunagh's daughter Elizabeth was getting married in Lincolnshire. Joan and I were invited. It proved to be a really exciting wedding. When we arrived I discovered that two of Lord De L'Isle's daughters were waiting to greet us – we had seen a lot of each other in Australia and they were part of the network that wove me together with the family. Joan was quite surprised to see how much affection the family and friends had for me. I was greeted enthusiastically and was amazed that we had been given seats in the chapel whilst many guests were listening to the wedding service from an array of seats outside in a marquee.

Elizabeth looked stunning wearing a family tiara, the diamonds sparkling in the light, and she and her husband-to-be Quintin looked the perfect couple as they took their places before the altar. Joan was used to taking weddings but was delighted to be part of a service where everyone sang the hymns so enthusiastically; realising that many of the men would have been used to singing well in their public school days.

We were treated to a delicious meal in the decorated marquee. Once again Joan was interested to see that we were very much part of the assembled guests – not put at the back of the room as 'staff.'

Nearly three years later Joan's telephone rang. It was Elizabeth ringing to say that her baby daughter, Eleanor, was shortly to be baptised and would we like to go to the baptismal service? Joan was really pleased but then lost for words when Elizabeth went on to say that it would take place in the Crypt of the House of Lords. This was possible because Quintin's parents, Lord Hailsham and Baroness Hailsham were members of the House of Lords. We knew it would be another exciting occasion as we prepared to get ready, with the necessary identity cards to give us entry.

We were invited to have lunch beforehand with Shaunagh and her parents, Romaine and Shaunagh's husband Crispin, together with Elizabeth's brother Harry and Crispin's three children, Sophia, Drummond and Rosie. It was a jolly party. We then went over to Westminster Hall, down the stone steps that led to the most beautiful chapel and baptistery you could ever want to see. There were wonderful paintings on the wall, the marble font decorated with gold and more paintings. There was so much for Eleanor to see that she hardly noticed she was being baptised. We felt very privileged once again to be part of such an eventful day.

Suddenly there was more exciting news to come. Joan's daughter Rachel told us that she was expecting a baby. She was on the last stretch of her training to become a consultant anaesthetist. Joan had always told her that she would help Rachel with childcare so that all the years of Rachel's training would not be wasted. There was a geographical snag though. Rachel and her husband Richard lived ten miles north of Cirencester, thirty-four miles from Joan's home in Wiltshire. After much thought and discussion Joan decided to sell her house and buy another in Cirencester so that she would be nearer to Rachel. She didn't relish the idea of driving sixty-eight miles each day in all weathers. We thought it would be good if I went with Joan to help with the baby - my nanny experiences might come in useful. So I also decided to move to Cirencester.

In the event Joan couldn't find a suitable house and I couldn't find an affordable flat. Richard's mother then said that she would like to share the care of the baby, which would mean that the two grandmothers could do two days each a week, while Rachel and Richard would fit in one other day. There was therefore no need for Joan to leave the house that she had lived in for over forty years. Perhaps I could find a flat in Baydon? Richard, Joan's son in New Zealand asked why I didn't move in with Joan as we spent so much time together. This was a great solution as we could then go together two days a week to look after the baby.

But it meant that I had to give up my flat, which had been my home for twenty-two years years. It was rented so that was no problem but I had to get rid of most of my possessions as Joan had a fully equipped house and had no need of all the things I had accumulated over the years. I just took with me my bed, a small sofa, some of my favourite pictures and most of my books.

Before I made the final decision to join Joan I rang Shaunagh. She is always behind me and ready with advice. She was lovely, she had met Joan a lot and was fond of her so had no worries but she gave me one piece of excellent advice 'Pack one large box with your tea-set, kettle, cups and saucers, iron and microwave and then if you ever had to leave you would have the basic requirements to start again.

I had all sorts of sales in which I sold some of my better pictures and china. I also gave much away to the homeless centres in Oxford who were always crying out for blankets and pillows and so on. I was also able to pass on some of my furniture to the young mother who was moving from a smaller flat into mine.

It was a wrench to leave behind all the friends I had made in the church I had attended and I would miss my Women's Institute friends, the charity coffee mornings and all those things that had made up my life in Oxford. I knew though that I would be able to go back quite regularly to see my friends again and importantly I would still be able to see my last lovely family – Lucy, Beth, Sam and Kate Brockie.

The Brockies were great and I had enjoyed over eleven years looking after the children. Andy and Janet, their parents, were very supportive of the work I did, but more crucially, of anything that concerned the children. They always put their needs first and seemed to have endless time and patience to give to the children, in spite of them both having demanding jobs. As I look at the growing family now I am filled with admiration. They have all done exceedingly well at school and on into their university careers and have an enviable relationship with each other.

Janet and Andy taught me how to manage the transition from the work I had done living in with families to working on a daily basis. On one hand I had been working with the family around me all day but now the parents left for work as soon as I arrived at their home and I left as soon as they came back in the evening. I was alone with the children in their home all day.

Nevertheless I was still part of their network, we were part of each other's lives and depended on each other and relied on each other, trusting each other. It felt good and is important to me now to have that sort of relationship with them. I owe them a lot.

During this period Joan discovered that it was possible for her to have a very new and complicated heart operation that would put an end to the problems she had been suffering for quite a few years. So it was her turn to go into hospital – the Heart Hospital in London. She underwent a procedure in which her heart was operated on partly by robots. She was conscious throughout and told us how weird it was to see the doctors controlling the operation on their computers. The operation was a success and thankfully she has a much better quality of life now.

Now it was my turn again, some years after I left the Brockies I began to have trouble with my knees, a true sign of old age approaching it seemed. After investigations I was advised to have a knee replacement, so once again was preparing to go into hospital, this time to the Nuffield Orthopaedic Centre in Oxford. I had a full replacement on one knee and later a partial replacement on the second knee. Both were straightforward operations, Joan was beside me to help with the recovery time. I was quite keen to become as mobile as I could as soon as I could so persevered with the exercises and managed to walk without sticks in five weeks, which was encouraging.

28 Matthew – in retirement

Another new phase was in store now. We were delighted when Rachel's baby was born – a little boy called Matthew- who was going to make a big difference in our lives. Rachel looked after him for seven months before returning to her work. We then found ourselves leaving home at 6.15am two or three days a week to drive to the Cotswolds to care for Matthew, getting to his home in time for his parents to leave for their work at 7.15am. They tried to get home by 6.30pm but sometimes they were held up and it would be 8 or 8.30 pm before we were back in Baydon. Quite a long day for us both.

Matthew took a little while to settle but as he got older he became a very charming, talkative little boy who has never ceased to entertain us. As I write he has just celebrated his fourth birthday, already attending a nursery school and lapping up any information that comes his way. He loves words; he began to talk very early and now has an incredibly extensive vocabulary and has an uncanny ability to fit the longest words he hears into their proper settings. Joan and I are continually surprised as we listen to him. It is an added blessing to have someone small in my life again on whom I can practise the skills I once used in my working days.

Except at holiday times our days are shorter with him now as we don't go until the afternoon to collect him from school. We wonder what life will have in store for him.

Just as everything was going along smoothly I slipped on ice a few days before Christmas in 2010 and broke my right femur. A true disaster as I upset everyone's plans for Christmas. I had the accident in the grounds of the John Radcliffe Hospital in Oxford just as I was on my way to deliver the Brockie children's Christmas presents. I had found the one section in the hospital car park where someone had perhaps been washing a car. Light snow had covered the black ice so I didn't notice it!

From the hospital I rang the Brockies so that they wouldn't wait for me. Within ten minutes Lucy and Sam were with me while I was being assessed, and saw me into the ward, looking quite concerned. Joan was travelling down from Sheffield with Chris so they diverted to Oxford, Chris bringing with him a new toothbrush and box of chocolates, which he picked up at a service station. Joan lent me her spongebag with some of the contents she thought I might need. I was so sorry for them. They were planning to go to Germany after Joan's busy time with church services over the Christmas period. I had spoilt all those plans as well as my own. I had planned to visit Shaunagh and Crispin in Spain.

I had a plate put into my leg and was sent home on Christmas Eve with instructions to hop for the next three months as I wasn't allowed to allow my leg to bear any weight! I had received some physiotherapy in the hospital but had very little chance of getting any help at home as no one in the health service seemed willing to take responsibility for me. I had the accident in Oxfordshire, we lived in Wiltshire and our GP was just over the border in West Berkshire so I fell between three stools. Eventually an occupational therapist came out and organised a stair rail and bath lift to use when I would be able to get upstairs. In the meantime I used Chris's downstairs bedroom with cloakroom next door and had to manage as best as I could with the ever faithful Joan looking after me.

It was a nightmare to get out of the house as I had to get over two steps at the front door. I couldn't hop over them but Joan devised a system. She put her piano stool over the first step, I sat on the stool then using my frame I hopped over while she ran through the house, out of the back door to meet me at the front door. An exhausting business! Our village shopkeeper lent me a wheelchair but it was too heavy for Joan to push, however Chris had a brainwave. Joan called me one day to look out of the window and there was Chris driving an electric wheelchair down the drive. He had bought it on Amazon and plans to sell it again when he is sure I won't need it. What friends Joan and Chris and my new family have been to me.

I found the wheelchair quite difficult to manage at first and really didn't enjoy going out in it. Our village paths are uneven and it seemed to be tipping me out. However in time I got the hang of it and was glad of it to get up to the shop for a change. We continued to have struggles to get any physiotherapy help despite the valiant efforts of our doctor but I persisted with the exercises I had been given at the hospital. After three months I was able to use a stick and am still using it fifteen months later when I go out, as my leg seems weaker than it used to be. Things obviously take longer to heal as you get older.

Sadly, while I was in hospital, I had news that my sister, Betty, had died. She had been very frail for a number of years but it was a blow to learn that she had died at the time when I couldn't get down to Kent to be with my brother-in-law and my two nephews. They wanted Joan to take the funeral service for Betty so it was doubly disappointing for her to have to decline. I have a very small family so it would have been especially important to be there with them. Betty's husband, Frank, included an obituary that I sent from hospital and his two sons, Graham and Stuart, supported him through it all.

As I write, my nephew Stuart has just finished walking 2,500 miles around the coast of England, to raise awareness of the need to talk about mental health problems. He took eight months off work as a maths teacher to achieve this aim, talking to various community groups and being interviewed on local radio stations as he passed round the country. He walked with his Springer Spaniel, Poppy, for company. His wife Kate and his brother Graham joined him from time to time to cheer him on, together with other friends who helped him on his way. His father and I joined his many supporters in reading his blog on Facebook every night.

Back in Baydon, the people here in the village have been really kind and welcoming. I seem to have been accepted and have absolutely no regrets in leaving Oxford as I have a good life here with Joan and her friends and her gorgeous family. The villagers have all been friendly and ready to stop and chat as we pass each other on our way to the shop. Joan and I have joined a travel group in Swindon, we go to local concerts and to any local events and I am very involved with the village church.

Two years ago I was persuaded to become one of the churchwardens in Baydon. I had done things to help in the church I attended in Oxford but never tackled anything as difficult as this and didn't really know what was expected of me. However I have managed to get through two years so far and only have one more year to go. I will have run out of puff by the end of a third year and will be pleased to hand over to someone younger.

The job has been complicated because water comes through the church roof whenever we have winds and rain together. We have to watch the weather forecast so as to put out bowls and buckets to catch the falling water. The lead was stolen from the roof many years ago and the covering that has been applied since has proved inadequate. We are now trying to raise £20,000 to have a permanent covering applied. That isn't an easy task with a small congregation and no lord of the manor to help, but the villagers are rallying round and supporting our fund-raising efforts and we hope to get the work done before I retire.

What is this retirement though? Will there ever be a time when I wonder how I am going to fill the hours in the day? Somehow I think there will always be something to do round the next corner, if past history is anything to go by, and to be quite honest – I like it that way.